Frommer's

Krakow
day BY day®

2nd Edition

by Peterjon Cresswell

WILEY

John Wiley & Sons, Inc.

Contents

Editorial Director: Kelly Regan
Production Manager: Daniel Mersey
Commissioning Editor: Jill Emeny
Development Editor: Jill Emeny
Content Editor: Erica Peters
Photo Research: Cherie Cincilla, Richard H. Fox, Jill Emeny
Cartography: Simonetta Giori

British Library Cataloguing in Publication Data
A catalogue record for this book is available from the British Library

ISBN 978-1-119-97021-7 (pbk), ISBN 978-1-119-97127-6 (ebk),
ISBN 978-1-119-97128-3 (ebk), ISBN 978-1-119-97129-0 (ebk)

Typeset by Wiley Indianapolis Composition Services
Printed and bound in China by RR Donnelley

5 4 3 2 1

A Note from the Editorial Director

Organizing your time. That's what this guide is all about.

Other guides give you long lists of things to see and do and then expect you to fit the pieces together. The Day by Day guides are different. These guides tell you the best of everything, and then they show you how to see it *in the smartest, most time-efficient way*. Our authors have designed detailed itineraries organized by time, neighborhood, or special interest. And each tour comes with a bulleted map that takes you from stop to stop.

Hoping to take a city tour by Trabant car, climb Wawel Cathedral's Zygmunt Tower for luck, or take a romantic moment on grassy slopes of the Vistula? Planning to bar hop around Plac Nowy, test out some of the city's new five-star restaurants, or disappear down a bewildering salt mine? Whatever your interest or schedule, the Day by Days give you the smartest routes to follow. Not only do we take you to the top attractions, hotels, and restaurants, but we also help you access those special moments that locals get to experience—those "finds" that turn tourists into travelers.

The Day by Days are also your top choice if you're looking for one complete guide for all your travel needs. The best hotels and restaurants for every budget, the greatest shopping values, the wildest nightlife—it's all here.

Why should you trust our judgment? Because our authors personally visit each place they write about. They're an independent lot who say what they think and would never include places they wouldn't recommend to their best friends. They're also open to suggestions from readers. If you'd like to contact them, please send your comments our way at feedback@frommers.com, and we'll pass them on.

Enjoy your Day by Day guide—the most helpful travel companion you can buy. And have the trip of a lifetime.

Warm regards,

Kelly Regan

Kelly Regan, Editorial Director
Frommer's Travel Guides

About the Author

Rescued from provincial misery by football and punk rock, German-born **Peterjon Cresswell** turned to Europe for work and inspiration. He has been on the road ever since. A graduate from the University of Westminster in Russian and French, he used long-term study trips in Provence, Kiev, a Russian monastery outside Paris and Leningrad to complete theses on the French football press and the underground music scene in the Soviet Union. After joining an English-language publication, *Budapest Week,* he has since spent the last 2 decades working freelance in the region, covering sport and travel in Poland, Croatia, Germany, and Slovenia. He also writes for the *Guardian,* the *Observer,* www.uefa.com, *World Soccer,* and a slew of in-flight magazines. *Krakow Day by Day* is his first book for Frommer's.

Acknowledgments

The author would like to thank Magdalena Osuch at the Krakow Tourism Office and the Art Hotel Niebieski.

Star Ratings, Icons & Abbreviations

Every hotel, restaurant, and attraction listing in this guide has been ranked for quality, value, service, amenities, and special features using a star-rating system. Hotels, restaurants, attractions, shopping, and nightlife are rated on a scale of zero stars (recommended) to three stars (exceptional). In addition to the **star-rating system,** we also use a **kids icon** to point out the best bets for families. Within each tour, we recommend cafes, bars, or restaurants where you can take a break. Each of these stops appears in a shaded box marked with a coffee-cup-shaped bullet ☕ .

The following **abbreviations** are used for credit cards:

AE	American Express	DISC	Discover	V	Visa
DC	Diners Club	MC	MasterCard		

Travel Resources at Frommers.com

Frommer's travel resources don't end with this guide. Frommer's website, **www.frommers.com**, has travel information on more than 4,000 destinations. We update features regularly, giving you access to the most current trip-planning information and the best airfare, lodging, and car-rental bargains. You can also listen to podcasts, connect with other Frommers.com members through our active-reader forums, share your travel photos, read blogs from guidebook editors and fellow travelers, and much more.

Advisory & Disclaimer

Travel information can change quickly and unexpectedly, and we strongly advise you to confirm important details locally before traveling, including information on visas, health and safety, traffic and transport, accommodations, shopping, and eating out. We also encourage you to stay alert while traveling, and to remain aware of your surroundings. Avoid civil disturbances, and keep a close eye on cameras, purses, wallets, and other valuables.

While we have endeavored to ensure that the information contained within this guide is accurate and up-to-date at the time of publication, we make no representations or warranties with respect to the accuracy or completeness of the contents of this work and specifically disclaim all warranties, including without limitation warranties of fitness for a particular purpose. We accept no responsibility or liability for any inaccuracy or errors or omissions, or for any inconvenience, loss, damage, costs, or expenses of any nature whatsoever incurred or suffered by anyone as a result of any advice, or information contained in this guide.

The inclusion of a company, organization or website in this guide as a service provider and/or potential source of further information does not mean that we endorse them or the information they provide. Be aware that information provided through some websites may be unreliable and can change without notice. Neither the publisher nor author shall be liable for any damages arising herefrom.

How to Contact Us

In researching this book, we discovered many wonderful places—hotels, restaurants, shops, and more. We're sure you'll find others. Please tell us about them, so we can share the information with your fellow travelers in upcoming editions. If you were disappointed with a recommendation, we'd love to know that, too. Please e-mail: frommers@wiley.com or write to:

Frommer's Krakow Day by Day, 2nd Edition
John Wiley & Sons, Inc. • 111 River St. • Hoboken, NJ 07030-5774

12 Favorite
Moments

12 Favorite Moments

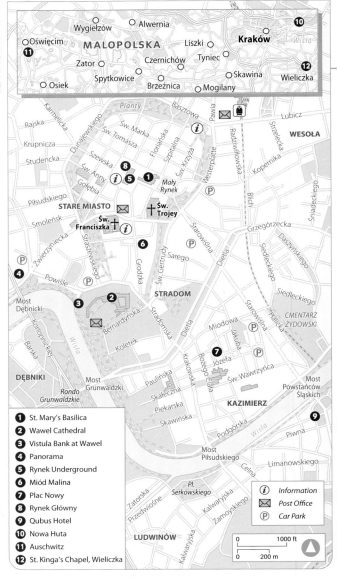

1. St. Mary's Basilica
2. Wawel Cathedral
3. Vistula Bank at Wawel
4. Panorama
5. Rynek Underground
6. Miód Malina
7. Plac Nowy
8. Rynek Główny
9. Qubus Hotel
10. Nowa Huta
11. Auschwitz
12. St. Kinga's Chapel, Wieliczka

ⓘ Information
✉ Post Office
Ⓟ Car Park

0 ____ 1000 ft
0 ____ 200 m

Previous page: Rynek Główny.

Charming, cultured, intimate Krakow is full of quirks and surprises. Who would have thought that a city with a stern historic center would have such wild nightlife, or that you can tour its sights by horse and trap or Trabant car? As the local economy booms, Krakow's new face is reflected in every recent five-star hotel and high-end restaurant. Here are my recommended moments to catch before the malls move in:

❶ Entering St. Mary's and gawping at the ceiling. Many line up daily for Veit Stoss' main altar, but the real pleasure lies in gazing up at the ceiling inside. After 600 years of war, plague, invasion, and occupation, these gold stars still twinkle, the firmament as blue as blue can be. Life-affirming every time. *See p 23*.

❷ Seeing the view of Krakow from the Zygmunt Tower. It's a big climb from inside Wawel Cathedral up the narrow staircase of the Zygmunt Tower—but so worth it. Stand under the clapper of the bell and touch it with your left hand for luck. *See p 53*.

❸ Canoodling on the grassy slopes of the Vistula. The grassy slopes below Wawel have an unspoiled view of the Vistula. Couples canoodle over a shared can of Zywiec beer and the evening brings promise of nearby adventure. *See p 85*.

❹ Sipping a sunset drink at the Panorama. The lift of the Jubilat shopping center whisks those in the know up to a retro club and restaurant with a terrace that offers cocktails and panoramic views. *See p 104*.

❺ Walking through history below the Cloth Hall. Krakow's best new attraction is the Rynek Underground museum, beneath the main square, where visitors learn about the daily life, trade, and culture of medieval Krakow through sounds, smells, and authentic artifacts. *See p 7*.

❻ Tucking into top Polish cuisine at a (reserved) window seat at Miód Malina. This is the perfect spot on the Royal Route to enjoy spare ribs in honey with the house plum sauce, or lamb chops in garlic and rosemary. Reliably delicious and affordable, your dish is delivered with a smile by Krakow's friendliest waiting staff. *See p 105*.

❼ Barhopping around Plac Nowy. This once grim market square now boasts a dozen bars, perfect from breakfast to bedtime. They range from French-themed to retro Communist, and one for an alternative music crowd. All are within 5 minutes' walk of one another. *See p 58*.

Rynek Underground.

Top Polish cuisine at Miód Malina.

Excellent dinner + two

⑧ Hearing the bugle play as you cross the market square (Rynek Główny) late at night. Four mournful refrains float out from each corner of St. Mary's tower day and night, whether you're shopping or clubbing. *See p 23.*

⑨ Sitting in the panoramic Jacuzzi atop the Qubus Hotel. The top floor of the swish Qubus comprises a glass-walled pool and Jacuzzi. Sit in the bubbles while gazing at the cityscape. *See p 143.*

⑩ Riding to Nowa Huta by Trabant. Krakow has tours by bike, buggy, and horse-driven carriage but nothing beats a trip to retro Nowa Huta by two-stroke Trabbie. Crazy Guides run tailored visits and your own driver will talk you through social and political history as you rattle through Krakow's streets. *See p 66.*

⑪ Seeing school groups diligently visit Auschwitz. Never again. This thought stays with you as you stand beneath these gates—*Arbeit Macht Frei*—contemplating the horrors perpetrated on the other side. School groups from across Europe stand at this same spot too, on a daily basis, before you're taken on a tour of the world's most notorious death camp. *See p 149.*

⑫ Descending the staircase of the Chapel of St. Kinga in Wieliczka. Halfway into a tour of Poland's most popular tourist attraction, the Salt Mine of Wieliczka outside Krakow, you reach this grand, shiny staircase, and ballroom-sized chapel below. Chandelier, altar, everything has been finely carved from rock salt by uneducated miners working for years underground. Ornate doesn't begin to describe it. *See p 20.* ●

Explore Krakow in a Crazy Guides Trabbie.

KKC 3497

1 The Best **Full-Day Tours**

The Best **in One Day**

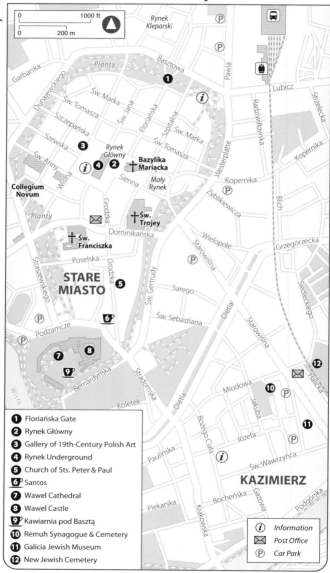

0 1000 ft	
0 200 m	

Rynek Kleparski

Planty

Garbarska

Dunajewskiego

Św. Marka

Szczepańska

Szewska

Św. Anny

Wiślna

Collegium Novum

Planty

Św. Tomasza

Św. Jana

Św. Marka

Floriańska

Szpitalna

Basztowa

Pawia

Lubicz

Westerplatte

Radziwiłłowska

Strzelecka

Kopernika

Rynek Główny

0 **0**

Sienna

Bazylika Mariacka

Mały Rynek

Kopernika

Zyblikiewicza

Blich

Grzegórzecka

Grodzka

Św. Trojey

Dominikańska

Wielopole

Starowiślna

Św. Franciszka

Poselska

STARE MIASTO

Straszewskiego

Grodzka

0

Św. Gertrudy

Sarego

Starowiślna

Siedleckiego

0

Św. Sebastiana

Dietla

Podzamcze

0 **0**

0

Bernardyńska

Stradomska

Wisła

Koletek

Dietla

Miodowa

Jakuba

0

Halicka

0

0

Józefa

0

Bożego Ciała

Paulińska

i

Św. Wawrzyńca

KAZIMIERZ

Piekarska

Bocheńska

Gazowa

Podgórska

Krakowska

1. Floriańska Gate
2. Rynek Główny
3. Gallery of 19th-Century Polish Art
4. Rynek Underground
5. Church of Sts. Peter & Paul
6. Santos
7. Wawel Cathedral
8. Wawel Castle
9. Kawiarnia pod Basztą
10. Remuh Synagogue & Cemetery
11. Galicia Jewish Museum
12. New Jewish Cemetery

i	Information
✉	Post Office
P	Car Park

Previous page: Church of Sts. Peter & Paul.

This 1-day tour takes in the very best of Krakow, in three key areas: The Old Town with its centerpiece of Rynek Główny, Europe's largest medieval square; historic hilltop Wawel, its cathedral and castle; and the atmospheric Jewish quarter of Kazimierz. Each zone is compact and walkable—the lesser landmarks you pass can be explored later at your leisure. START: **All trams to Barbakan.**

Floriańska Gate, the entrance to the Old Town.

❶ Floriańska Gate. Enter Krakow like a king as you pass through this medieval entrance to the Old Town, one of four to survive from the original 47 built in the 1300s. The gate forms the start of the Royal Route up to Wawel, marched by Polish monarchs and now signposted for tourists. Linked to the 15th-century **Barbican** bastion adjoining the tram-lined ring road around the Old Town, the Floriańska Gate bears the eagle of the Piast dynasty, rulers when the fortification was constructed. After a quick peek at the artworks mounted on the walls, join the throng down busy Floriańska up to Rynek Główny, the main market square. ⏱ *10 min. All trams to Barbakan.*

❷ ★★★ kids Rynek Główny. Take a deep breath as you arrive at Europe's largest medieval square— the spiritual center of Krakow and the rallying point for Polish independence when the nation was off the map. Thankfully intact after World War II, this masterpiece of design and symmetry is strolled around by thousands of people every day. At its heart stands the **Sukiennice** (p 78), the former **Cloth Hall,** now an indoor

Rynek Główny is Europe's largest medieval square.

Detail on the Church of Sts. Peter & Paul.

market lined with souvenir stands. Around the square are cafe and restaurant terraces, fashion stores, and historic facades—you'll feel the urge to linger over a beer. Landmarks include **St. Mary's Basilica** (p 23), the Town Hall Tower, and the **Kryzsztofory Palace** (p 23), housing the History Museum. Note, too, the new attractions of the Gallery of 19th-Century Polish Art in the Sukiennice (p 24) and the Rynek Underground historical walk-through beneath it. Tourist carriages clip-clop on the cobblestones, the only transportation allowed here. 🕐 *1 hr. See p 23.*

3 ★ Gallery of 19th-Century Polish Art. Opened in 2010 after a 3-year renovation, this attractive museum occupies the upper floor of the Sukiennice. Over four rooms, the collection covers a pivotal century of Polish art, with a mixture of portraits, landscapes, and scenes from Polish history. Each room is named after a particular artist and theme. 🕐 *1½ hr. See p 24* **6**.

4 ★★★ kids Rynek Underground. Easily the best attraction to open in Krakow for a long time, this extensive and imaginative recreation of how life was down the centuries around the main square and in the Old Town, is based on actual finds from the long-term archaeological digs here. Expect long lines in the holiday season. 🕐 *1½ hr. See p 26,* **8**.

5 ★ Church of Sts. Peter & Paul. The Royal Route continues from the southeast corner of Rynek Główny to Grodzka, wide, historic, and diverse. Halfway down the street, near the junction with Kanonicza, stands a cluster of churches. Your eye will be drawn to the most striking, the first Jesuit—and baroque—church in Krakow. Italian architects were brought over to build it in the early 1600s and, like all Jesuit churches, it is modeled on Il Gesù in Rome. Inside, the delicate stuccowork and high altar, added a century later, impress but first you'll be snapping the statues of the 12 Apostles interspersed amid the railings guarding the main entrance—copies of the 18th-century originals. To one side, steps lead to the Skarga Crypt, named after the Jesuit preacher whose tombstone is dotted with wishes written by locals needing help in sundry everyday tasks. 🕐 *20 min.*

Snap Happy

Photos: Entering many of Krakow's churches, museums, and historic attractions, the first-time visitor may not notice a special ticket price indicated at the kiosk. Buying a standard ticket and innocently snapping away happily at a rare altar or painting, said visitor may be apprehended by a steward in a luminous top—the taking of photographs requires this special ticket, usually about 7 zł extra. Once you've been led to the desk to buy one, you can snap away at random, send the photos to friends, post them on your blog, or show them on your living-room wall. What you can't do is publish them—the Wawel authorities are particularly scrupulous when it comes to unauthorized publication of photographs.

Grodzka 52a. ☎ 012/350-63-65. www.apostolowie.pl. Mon–Sat 9am–7pm; Sun 1:30–7:30pm. All trams to Pl.Wszystkich Świętych/Św.Gertrudy.

6 **kids** **Santos.** Ideally situated at the bottom end of Grodzka with its tree-shaded terrace facing Wawel, this modest cafe and purveyor of standard snacks and decent ice creams provides an ideal pit-stop for those following the Royal Route. Grodzka 65. ☎ 012/423-14-87. zł.

7 ★★★ **Wawel Cathedral.**
From the bottom of Grodzka, Wawel rises stern and historic. This fortified complex contains Poland's most precious landmarks, Wawel Castle and Cathedral, royal residence and coronation site for generations of Polish monarchs. After a steep incline and two gates, you arrive at the cathedral on your left, its ticket office opposite the main entrance. Following the arrows as you enter, your eyes are assaulted by a mass of objects and an array of styles, bright chapels, ornate tombs, and sarcophagi flanking the three-aisled nave. On the left-hand side is the entrance to the crypt, containing the tombs of Polish rulers and

national heroes; further along is the **Zygmunt Tower.** Climb the narrow, steep, and claustrophobic staircase for panoramic views of Krakow. The clapper of the **Zygmunt Bell,** 2m (6.5 ft.) in diameter, is only used for special occasions—reach up to touch it with your left hand for luck. ⏱ 1½ hr. See p 53, **1**.

8 ★★★ **kids** **Wawel Castle.**
Turning left out of the Cathedral, a short walk leads you to an elegantly arcaded Renaissance courtyard, surrounded on three sides by an Italianate building crammed with historic treasures: Wawel Castle.

The historic Wawel Cathedral.

Wawel Castle courtyard.

Boys will enjoy the brutal medieval weaponry on show in **the Crown Treasury** and **Armory;** grownups the Flemish tapestries in the **State Rooms** and **Royal Private Apartments,** accessed by guided tour only. All is housed in expansive, high-ceilinged, interconnecting rooms overlooking the courtyard. As tourists shuffle in and out of this east wing, you'll see New Age practitioners making strange movements

Kawiarnia pod Basztą.

in the northwest corner. The black stone of the former **St. Gereon's Chapel,** whose remnants are set behind the wall, is said to emanate positive energy. Facing the outer courtyard is the entrance to the medieval finds of the Lost Wawel exhibition (7 zł adults, 4 zł children); further on is the door to the child-friendly **Dragon's Cave** (p 34), a labyrinth bookended by a roaring dragon. ⏱ *1½ hr. See p 54,* ❹.

❾ kids **Kawiarnia pod Basztą.** Take a terrace seat to face the morning sun under Tęczyński Tower. Breakfasts, soups, sandwiches, pancakes, cakes, ice creams, standard Polish lunches, beers, and spirits are served at Wawel's main cafe. There's a children's menu (13 zł) too. *Wzgórze Wawelskie 9.* ☎ *012/422 7528. zł.*

❿ ★★ **Remuh Synagogue & Cemetery.** Down Stradomska from Wawel you arrive at the Jewish quarter of Kazimierz. No longer in the Old Town, you quickly sense a different culture, its rich history and its tragic wartime loss. Turning into Miodowa, synagogues begin to spring up; a little turn into broad, square-like Szeroka and to your right is the gateway to the Remuh Synagogue and Cemetery. Founded in the 1500s and renovated in 1829, this is the only Orthodox one in Krakow still running regular religious services—Torah readings are given from the traditional bimah platform. As you exit, to your left stretches the rambling Remuh Cemetery, with the Wailing Wall immediately to the right. The inscriptions are hard to read—many gravestones were damaged when the Nazis used this for a rubbish tip. Pebbles are left on top as a mark of respect. ⏱ 1 hr. See p 38, **1**.

Decorative screen in the Remuh Synagogue.

11 ★★ Galicia Jewish Museum. British photojournalist Chris Schwarz and writer-historian Jonathan Webber recorded the wartime scenes of murder and massacre around southern Poland (Galicia). These ghostly images are displayed in this intelligent and worthwhile museum, reflecting the breadth and banality of crimes committed mainly by locals. ⏱ 30 min. See p 40, **6**.

12 ★★ New Jewish Cemetery. After the Austrians closed the main

Remuh Cemetery in 1800, this rambling site, Krakow's largest Jewish cemetery, was opened. Set to the east of the main hub of the Jewish quarter, over the railway tracks from Starowiślna, this is also the only one of its kind still in operation today. By the entrance stands a monument to Jews murdered during World War II, built with broken tombstones. ⏱ 45 min. See p 40, **7**.

Pretzel Logic

Pretzels: If you're starting the day on or around the main square, you're bound to find a little glassed-in stand selling fresh *obwarzanki,* a kind of local pretzel. Priced at about 1.30 zł and usually available in plain, sesame, or poppy-seed varieties, they provide a cheap, filling, and easy-to-carry snack as you wander around the Old Town. For those with two or three kids in tow, it's the ideal solution for mid-morning hunger. Try to buy them first thing in the morning, as by late afternoon they can be pretty brittle!

The Best **in Two Days**

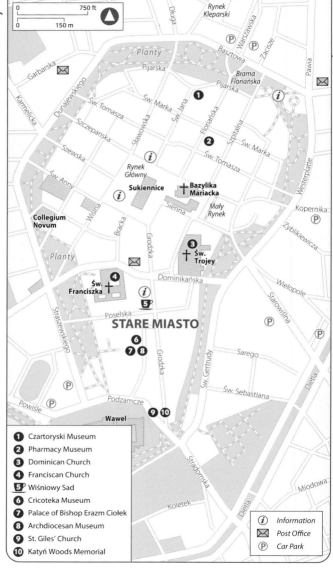

0 — 750 ft
0 — 150 m

Długa
Rynek
Kleparski
Warszawska
Basztowa
Zacisze
Pawia
Planty
Pijarska
Garbarska
Brama
Floriańska
Pijarska
Karmelicka
Dunajewskiego
Sw. Tomasza
Sw. Marka
Sw. Jana
Floriańska
Szpitalna
Sw. Marka
Szczepańska
Sławkowska
Sw. Tomasza
Westerplatte
Szewska
Rynek
Główny
Sw. Anny
Sukiennice
**Bazylika
Mariacka**
Kopernika
Wiślna
Sienna
Mały
Rynek
Zyblikiewicza
**Collegium
Novum**
Bracka
Grodzka
Planty
**Św.
Trojey**
Straszewskiego
Dominikańska
Wielopole
Starowiślna
**Św.
Franciszka**
Poselska
STARE MIASTO
Sarego
Sw. Gertrudy
Sw. Sebastiana
Dietla
Powiśle
Podzamcze
Stradomska
Wawel
Koletek
Miodowa
Dietla

❶	Czartoryski Museum
❷	Pharmacy Museum
❸	Dominican Church
❹	Franciscan Church
❺	Wiśniowy Sad
❻	Cricoteka Museum
❼	Palace of Bishop Erazm Ciołek
❽	Archdiocesan Museum
❾	St. Giles' Church
❿	Katyń Woods Memorial

ⓘ	Information
✉	Post Office
Ⓟ	Car Park

Your second day takes you right through the Old Town from top to bottom, around the historic streets of Floriańska, Grodzka, and Kanonicza, part of the Royal Route to Wawel. On the way, you'll be taking in the life and works of Leonardo da Vinci (1452–1519), Pope John Paul II (1920–2005), and Tadeusz Kantor (1915–90), Poland's legendary stage designer. START: **All trams to Old Town.**

1 ★★★ **Czartoryski Museum.** One of Krakow's most remarkable museums contains Da Vinci's *Lady with an Ermine*, Spanish, Venetian, and Flemish pieces, and military paraphernalia from all over Europe. Closed for renovation from 2010, due to reopen in 2012. ⏲ *1½ hr. See p 45,* **1**.

2 ★★ kids **Pharmacy Museum.** The quirky, surprising Pharmacy Museum fills this 15th-century building, each floor representing an apothecary from a particular century. You'll get a better feel here for how locals lived than at any other standard museum. ⏲ *1 hr. See p 45,* **2**.

3 ★ **Dominican Church.** Of all the churches in Krakow, the Dominican attracts the most faithful congregation—mass here really is a thing to behold. Founded by the Dominicans in 1250, this pretty mishmash of a church is a late 19th-century rebuild of the 13th-century

Czartoryski Museum.

Gothic original. Look out for the **Myszkowski Chapel,** its dome dotted with family busts. ⏲ *30 min. See p 47,* **7**.

Dominican Church.

Stunning detail from the Palace of Bishop Erazm Ciołek.

④ ★ Franciscan Church. Fire, fashion, and Swedish invasions are responsible for the varied architectural styles of this large church and cloisters. For its nearly 8 centuries of history, with baroque, neo-Romanesque, and neo-Gothic aspects, the Franciscan Church is best known for the interior work of Stanisław Wyspiański (1869–1907). Light floods in through the Art Nouveau forms of his stained-glass creations on each of the north and south wings—flowers, stars, and swirling patterns against a blue background. He was also responsible for the murals in the choir. Portraits of every Krakow bishop to the present day line the Gothic cloister. ⏱ 30 min. Wszystkich Świętych 5. ☎ 012/422-53-76. www.franciszkanska.pl. Mon–Sat 9:45am–4:15pm, Sun 1:15–4:15pm. All trams to Pl.Wszystkich Świętych/Św.Gertrudy.

⑤ Wiśniowy Sad. Russian specialties—borscht, *solyanka* (a rich, spicy stew), blini with caviar—complement a decent range of chilled vodkas at the Cherry Orchard, accessed down a quaint Grodzka passageway. *Grodzka 33.* ☎ 012/430-21-11. zlzł.

⑥ ★ Cricoteka Museum. The former home of Tadeusz Kantor's groundbreaking theater Cricot 2 now contains an eclectic archive of his work—to call it a museum is doing it an injustice. The costumes, videos, drawings, designs, journals, and photos all testify to the craft and imagination of Poland's greatest stage designer of the 20th century. Kantor himself put the house together before his death in 1990, a legacy in the "minds and imagination for the coming generations." For those unfamiliar with his work, it's the range of materials that strikes most—every Kantor production must have been a complete surprise. ⏱ 20 min. Kanonicza 5. ☎ 012/422-83-32. www.cricoteka.pl. Free admission. Mon, Wed, Thurs, Fri 10am–2pm; Tues 2pm–6pm. All trams to Pl.Wszystkich Świętych/Św.Gertrudy.

⑦ ★ Palace of Bishop Erazm Ciołek. Overhauled and reopened, this two-part collection covers the first era of a panoramic overview of Polish art—the 18th- and 19th-century section (currently under renovation) is at the Sukiennice (p 24), the 20th at the National Museum (p 31, ⑧). Here, in the sumptuous early 16th-century palace of canon, diplomat, and arts patron Bishop Erazm Ciołek, you'll find a gallery of Old Polish art between the 12th- and 18th-centuries, and another of

Orthodox art. The former features the late 15th-century Gothic works of **Veit Stoss** (ca. 1445–1533), responsible for the High Altar at St. Mary's Basilica (p 23), and ecclesiastical works of the Renaissance and baroque periods. The highlights are the icons of Ruthenia, the Balkans, and 17th-century Poland, vibrant Byzantine images of Christ and the Virgin. ⏰ *40 min. Kanonicza 17.* ☎ *012/424-93-85. www.muzeum.krakow.pl. Admission (combined) 20 zł adults, 10 zł children; old Polish collection 12 zł adults, 6 zł children; Orthodox collection 6 zł adults, 3 zł children. Free admission Sun. Tues–Sat 10am–6pm, Sun 10am–4pm. All trams to Pl.Wszystkich Świętych/Św. Gertrudy.*

8 ★ Archdiocesan Museum. The life, work, and travels of Pope John Paul II are the main subject here—temporary exhibitions of church art are often staged as well. Upstairs begins with a map of Papal pilgrimages, moving on to his skull caps, cloaks, amateur paintings, airline schedules, bicycles, and even his canoe. A goalkeeper for local soccer club Cracovia, John Paul was a man of sport too. Gifts from around the world are also on display: Salvers, figurines, and a beautifully hand-painted chess set from the President of Uruguay. There's also a reconstruction of the room he lived in while working here—the original is in the adjoining Deanery. ⏰ *20 min. Kanonicza 19.* ☎ *012/421-89-63. www.muzeumkra.diecezja.pl. Admission 5 zł adults, 3 zł children. Tues–Fri 10am–4pm, Sat–Sun 10am–3pm. All trams to Pl.Wszystkich Świętych/Św. Gertrudy.*

9 ★ St. Giles' Church. The last stop on the Royal Route before Wawel, St. Giles' has a rather patchwork history. Founded in 1082, it was rebuilt in the early 1300s and acquired its present appearance in the early 1600s. An English-language Catholic mass is given here on Sunday mornings; many visit for the summer concerts too. The Krakow Chamber Orchestra are regular performers. ⏰ *15 min. Św.Idziego 1. Free admission. Concert prices vary. All trams to Pl.Wszystkich Świętych/Św.Gertrudy.*

10 Katyń Woods Memorial. Erected in 1990, the crucifix in the cobbled square outside St. Giles' reads: "Katyń 1940–1990." The mass execution of 20,000 Polish officers and policemen by Stalin in the Katyń Woods near Smolensk was covered up for decades. By the late 1980s, the Soviet leader Mikhail Gorbachev was under pressure to admit Soviet guilt —acknowledged on April 13 1990, the anniversary of the discovery of the mass graves by the Nazis in 1943. This stark memorial crucifix was erected afterward. The tragedy was given added resonance in 2010 when a plane carrying the Polish president and nearly 90 politicians and high-ranking officers from Poland crashed in Smolensk. The officials were on their way to a 70th-anniversary ceremony of the Katyń massacre. ⏰ *15 min. Św.Idziego.*

Archdiocesan Museum.

The Best **in Three Days**

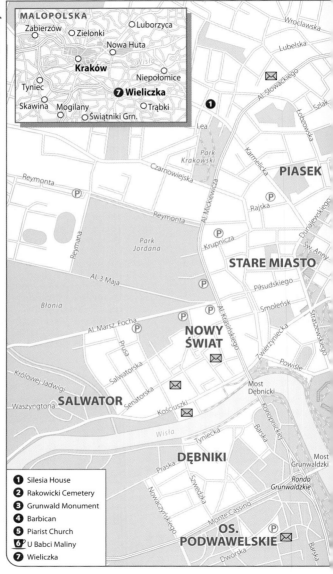

1 Silesia House
2 Rakowicki Cemetery
3 Grunwald Monument
4 Barbican
5 Piarist Church
6 U Babci Maliny
7 Wieliczka

Fort Kleparz
ⓟ Kamienna

NOWY KLEPARZ
Helclów

❷ Cmentarz Rakowicki

| 0 | 1000 ft |
| 0 | 200 m |

ⓘ Information
✉ Post Office
ⓟ Car Park

Długa
Szlak

Warszawska

Rakowicka

Al. Beliny-Prazmowskiego
Moniuszki
Kielecka

✉ Rynek Kleparski
Planty
❸
❺ ❹
Baszowa

ⓟ ⓟ
🚌
ⓟ
🚈
Pawia

Lubomirskiego
Topolowa

Rondo Mogilskie
Mogilska

Św. Marka
❻

ⓘ
Florańska
Szpitalna
Westerplatte
Radziwiłłowska
Lubicz

GRZEGÓRZKI

WESOŁA

Rynek Główny
ⓘ
Mały Rynek

Kopernika

Ogród Botaniczny
ⓟ

Al. Powstania Warszawskiego
Sądowa
ⓟ

✝ Św. Trojey
✉
✝ Św. Franciszka

Blich

Śniadeckiego

Grzegórzecka

Al. Pokoju

Grodzka
Św. Gertrudy
Sarego
Starowiślna
ⓟ
Dietla
ⓟ

Daszyńskiego
Siedleckiego

Rondo Grzegórzeckie

Kotlarska

STRADOM

Wawel

Bernardyńska
Stradomska
Dietla
Krakowska
Miodowa
Jakuba

Starowiślna
Halicka

Cmentarz Żydowski

Podgórska

Most Kotlarski

Koletek
Plac Nowy
Bożego Ciała
Józefa

Zabłocie

Paulińska

Piekarska
Plac Wolnica

Skawińska

Św. Wawrzyńca

KAZIMIERZ

Most Powstańców Śląskich

Na Zjeździe

Lipowa

Podgórska
Wisła
Piwna

Most Piłsudskiego
Limanowskiego
Celna

Day three starts north of the Old Town with sights relating to recent and not-too-recent history. Skirt the pretty Planty (p 89) and erudite University Quarter (p 49) to explore a couple of Krakow's most attractive and unusual churches. From the Hotel Cracovia west of the Old Town, tourist buses leave for Wieliczka, a unique underground labyrinth lined with statues made completely from salt—the most popular visitor attraction in Poland. **START: All trams to Pl.Inwalidów.**

1 ★★ **Silesia House.** An unprepossessing building by the northwest corner of Krakow's outer ring road, this was the Gestapo headquarters during the war. From the outer wall, hands reach out from prison bars, a striking sculpture set by the main gate into a nondescript courtyard. Press the bell immediately to your right and someone skips down from one of the flats to lead you into a basement. You're handed an English-language text and shown four tiny rooms—torture cells, with the original graffiti still

Grunwald Monument on Matejki Square.

carved on the walls, desperate messages ("21.XI.1944—fifth day of beating"), left behind after 65 years. Upstairs, a more conventional exhibition displays the activities of the Jewish Fighting Organization (ŻOB) and other Resistance movements. Chilling and unmissable. ⏱ *30 min. Ul.Pomorska 2.* ☎ *012/633-14-14. www.mhk.pl. Admission 6 zł adults, 5 zł children. Free admission Tues. Apr–Oct Tues–Sun 10am–5:30pm; Nov–Apr Tues, Wed, Fri 9am–4pm, Thurs noon–7pm, Sat–Sun 10am– 5pm. All trams to Pl.Inwalidów.*

2 **Rakowicki Cemetery.** Krakow's biggest cemetery occupies a vast tract just north of the main train station, a treasure of 19th-century funerary architecture and the resting place of some of Poland's greatest figures: 19th-century artists Józef Mehoffer (1869–1946) and Jan Matejko (1838–93), wartime Ghetto pharmacist Tadeusz Pankiewicz (1908–93), and 20th-century theater director Tadeusz Kantor, they're all here. If you're in town around All Souls' Day, November 1, a visit here is memorable, candles in translucent colored vases creating halos of light all around. ⏱ *1 hr. Ul.Rakowicka. Tram 2: Rakowicka n/z.*

3 **Grunwald Monument.** Ten minutes' walk toward the Old Town, this imposing depiction of Poland's greatest victory on the battlefield is a copy of the 1910 original, which was demolished by the Nazis. For

Germans, Grunwald is Tannenberg, the great military defeat for the Teutonic Knights at the hands of Poland and Lithuania 500 years before this monument was unveiled. The figures dramatically arrayed are the victorious King Jagiella and the fallen Teutonic leader, surrounded by knights and soldiers. Centerpiecing Plac Matejki, the work aligns neatly with Barbican and the Royal Route down Floriańska. ⏱ *10 min. Pl.Matejki. All trams to Dworzec Główny.*

❹ ★ **Barbican.** Fears of Turkish invasion led to the construction of this once mighty fortress and drawbridge in the late 1400s. Surrounded by a huge moat, the Barbican was never put to its original use—the Turks never came. The seven turrets and loopholes arranged at various levels are said to relate to astrological symbolism popular at the time. Today its grassed-over surrounds allow for a pleasant stroll into the Old Town from the north, linked to the Floriańska Gate (p 7) and the shopping stretch of Floriańska. The Barbican is used for exhibitions, concerts, and a festival of classical music in June. ⏱ *20 min. Basztowa. All trams to Basztowa.*

❺ ★ **Piarist Church.** A grand rococo facade and an equally ornate baroque interior with *trompe l'oeil* frescoes add an Italianate touch to this church at the far end of Floriańska—designer Kasper Bażanka was trained in Rome under Andrea Pozzo, Jesuit virtuoso of the illusionist mural. At Easter, the crypt is opened to display an intricate model of Christ's Tomb, usually with contemporary undertones. ⏱ *20 min. Pijarska 2.* ☎ *012/422-22-55. Free admission. All trams to Basztowa.*

The Barbican.

Piarist Church.

6 U Babci Maliny. A favorite place for locals to fill-up on *pierogi* (Slavic dumplings). Cheap, hearty helpings of doughballs of various fillings are served 7 days a week in a rustic basement. *Ul.Stawkowska 17.* ☎ *012/422-76-01. www.kuchniau babcimaliny.pl. zł.*

7 ★★★ kids Wieliczka. Poland's busiest tourist site means line-ups outside the main building and a wait for the 36-person lift to come rattling up to ground level, even if you've booked a timed guided tour from Krakow. Your visit to the Wieliczka mine lasts a few hours, through a labyrinth of corridors, where salt was mined for centuries. Exhibits cover mining techniques and equipment, and the figures intricately carved by the miners during their years underground. Most notable is the **Chapel of St. Kinga,** a 400-sq.m (4,305-sq. ft.) hall accessed down a (slippery) grand staircase, lit by a vast chandelier. Occasionally the tour lapses into kitsch—Chopin playing to a light show—but Wieliczka proves a winner with all the family. Be prepared to descend a lot of stairs. ⏲ *2 hr. Ul.Daniłowicza 10, Wieliczka.* ☎ *012/278-73-02. www. kopalnia.pl. Admission English-language 68 zł adults, 54 zł children. Daily Apr–Oct 7:30am–7:30pm; Nov–Mar 8am–5pm. All trains/minibuses to Wieliczka or by regular guided tour.* ●

Rynek Główny

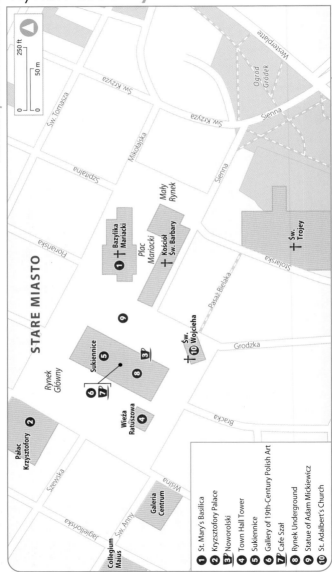

STARE MIASTO

Rynek Główny

Sukiennice

Wieża Ratuszowa

Bazylika Mariacki

Plac Mariacki

Kościół Św. Barbary

Mały Rynek

Św. Wojcieha

Św. Trojey

Pałac Krzysztofory

Galeria Centrum

Collegium Maius

- ❶ St. Mary's Basilica
- ❷ Krysztofory Palace
- 3 Noworolski
- ❹ Town Hall Tower
- ❺ Sukiennice
- ❻ Gallery of 19th-Century Polish Art
- 7 Cafe Szal
- ❽ Rynek Underground
- ❾ Statue of Adam Mickiewicz
- ❿ St. Adalbert's Church

Previous page: Vistula waterfront.

Mercifully untouched by war or 1970s' developers, the main market square of Rynek Główny glitters from all four sides with the grand neoclassical facades of the 18th and 19th centuries. Towering over the flagstone surface are four historic buildings including the standout Gothic St. Mary's Basilica and its historic high altar, and surrounding them, two dozen terrace cafes, restaurants, and upmarket boutiques. START: **All trams to Old Town.**

1 ★★★ **St. Mary's Basilica.** The jewel in Krakow's crown and one of the great works of the Gothic era, St. Mary's is fronted by two towers. The taller tower bears a spire and attracts everyone's attention on the hour when a trumpeter plays a bugle call four times, a tradition dating back to the Tatar invasion of 1241. Get your ticket from the office opposite the visitors' entrance round the corner on **Plac Mariacki** and find a pew beneath the blue-starred ceiling by 11:50am (not Sun), before the six hinged wings of Veit Stoss' masterful **High Altar** (1477–89) are unfolded for their daily public view. Some 1m (3.3 ft.) long and 12m (40 ft.) high, the altar is huge, its central section painstakingly depicting the *Assumption of the Virgin.* The realistic features on the faces of the Apostles are uncanny—the young Stoss was said to have taken them from real-life characters. The wings show scenes from Christ's life—the Nativity, Resurrection, and so on. The most prominent Polish artists of the 19th century were responsible for many of the stained-glass designs and murals in the nave. 🕐 *1 hr. Pl.Mariacki 5.* ☎ *012/422-05-21. Admission 6 zł adults, 3 zł children. Mon–Sat 11:30am–6pm, Sun 2–6pm. Arrive Mon–Sat before 11:40am for the altar opening at 11:50am. All trams to Old Town.*

2 ★ **Kryzsztofory Palace.** The grand Christopher Palace owes its present appearance to a remodel in the 1680s. Frequented by various cultural societies over the years, it is best known for hosting meetings of influential post-war artists, the Grupa Krakowska. Today its main function is to accommodate the **History Museum of Krakow,** whose worthwhile permanent collection remains under renovation until 2012. Temporary shows still run, though, with varied and interesting themes. 🕐 *40 min. Rynek Główny 35.* ☎ *012/619-23-00. www.mhk.pl. Admission 8 zł adults, 5 zł children. Wed–Sun 10am–5:30pm. All trams to Old Town.*

3 **Noworolski.** You won't find a more inspiring spot to write your postcards than this grand cafe, tucked in the Sukiennice. With outdoor tables in its arcades, it has seen many a famous regular—Lenin

The stunning ceiling in St. Mary's Basilica.

for one. The sumptuous fin-de-siècle interior gives you the impression of sitting inside a wedding cake—decoration, location, and heritage allowing the management to charge three times the going rate for coffee. Breakfasts, salads, cakes, soups, and main courses are all quite reasonably priced on the terrace, though. *Rynek Główny 1/3.* ☎ *012/422-47-71. złzł.*

④ ★ Town Hall Tower. Once part of a 14th-century town hall, the remaining tower has been converted into a modest museum and simple main-square attraction. A model of the original town hall and vintage photographs from the Old Town form the bulk of the exhibition, but most come here to scale the giddying 100-step staircase for a birds'-eye view of the square below. Outside at street level, a plaque marks where Colonel Bolesław Roja claimed power from the Austrian authorities in 1918, thus gaining Poland independence after 123 years. ◷ *20 min. Rynek Główny 1.* ☎ *012/619-23-20. Admission adults 7 zł, children 5 zł. May–Oct Daily 10:30am–6pm. Closed Nov–Apr. All trams to Old Town.*

Climb the town hall tower for a bird's eye view of Rynek Główny.

⑤ ★ Sukiennice. Rynek Główny's centerpiece has been a place of trade for 7 centuries but where artisans once cut cloth, now traders purvey souvenirs and overpriced jewelry. Nonetheless the building itself, given a neo-Gothic makeover, colonnades and all, in the 1870s, beckons you to walk through and browse with scores of other tourists. Two major attractions now feature here: The Gallery of 19th-Century Polish Art upstairs, and the Rynek Underground below street level. ◷ *20 min.*

⑥ ★ Gallery of 19th-Century Polish Art. Opened in 2010 after a 3-year renovation, this attractive museum occupies an entire floor of the Sukiennice. In four rooms, each named after a particular artist and theme, the collection covers a pivotal century of Polish art: Bacciarelli, the Enlightenment; Michałowski, Romanticism; Siemiradzki, Academicism; Chełmoński, Realism, Polish Impressionism, and Early Symbolism. The works feature a mixture of portraits, landscapes, and scenes from Polish history. Note the huge *Chełmoński* piece, Czwórka, in Room IV, and equally striking *Kościuszko at Racławice* by Jan Matejko in Room 3. Cloakroom use is obligatory and the cafe has perhaps the best view in all Krakow. ◷ *1½ hr. Sukiennice, Rynek Główny 3.* ☎ *012/424-46-03. www. muzeum.krakow.pl. Admission 12 zł adults, 6 zł children. Tues–Sun 10am–8pm. All trams to Old Town.*

⑦ Cafe Szał. The cafe of the Gallery of 19th-Century Polish Art is almost worth the museum entrance alone, for its terrace overlooking Krakow's main square from above. With a perfect view of St. Mary's Basilica, it offers a variety of fruit shakes, coffee with Bailey's or Kahlua, cakes, salads, and dinky *tramezzini* sandwiches. *Rynek Główny 3.* ☎ *012/424-46-03. złzł.*

Rynek Underground

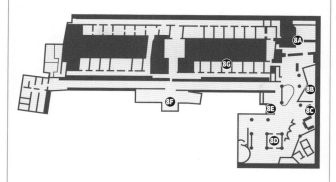

Walking through the image curtain of **medieval street scenes** at **8A**, visitors are greeted with a large model map of the main European trade routes, illustrating how important international exchange was to Krakow's development. Alongside **8B** is a thick slab of **authentic medieval cobblestone** found beneath the Sukiennice immediately above you many of the displays you will see are the result of the long-term archaeological dig here that started in 2005. Hair clips, spoons, fishing hooks, shoes, and combs are also laid out, used by some local Cracovian or other hundreds of years ago. You then follow reconstructions of **medieval workshops** **8C**—goldsmiths, blacksmiths—with all their attendant sounds around you. A detailed **model of the city** **8D** as it was in 1500 shows the layout of the Old Town, which appears

little different from what you might already recognize. A popular stop-off is the **medieval merchant's stall** **8E**, where you can weigh yourself according to five of the main systems of measurement 500 years ago: Krakow, London, Cologne, France, and Flanders. Once you've printed out your weight, you can check your height against your medieval counterparts. Continue on down a long corridor of **traders' stalls** **8F** that would have operated within the Sukiennice. Dotted around the place are **alcoves** **8G** showing televised historical reconstructions, with English subtitles. ⏱ 1½ hr. Rynek Główny 1. ☎ 012/426-50-04. www.podziemiarynku. com. Admission 13 zł adults, 10 zł children. Mon, Wed–Sun 10am–8pm, Tues 10am–4pm. Closed 1st Tues of the month. All trams to Old Town.

Buy your souvenirs at Sukiennice.

❽ ★★★ kids Rynek Underground. There are long lines outside this superb new attraction, set right beneath the city's main square. Rynek Underground is an extensive and imaginative recreation of Krakow life in (mainly) medieval times, based on actual finds from the long-term archaeological digs here. Visitors begin their journey by walking through an image curtain of street life, and follow around five main areas, dealing with trade, transportation, settlement, and so on. Touch screens in seven languages help guide you.

❾ Statue of Adam Mickiewicz. Mickiewicz never came to Krakow but Poland's national poet has been awarded a crucial role in the daily life of the city—his statue outside the Sukiennice is the most popular meeting place in Krakow. The monument is in fact a remake, the original having been destroyed in World War II, and has allegorical figures sitting at the feet of the man responsible for the greatest poetic epic of Polish letters, *Pan Tadeusz*. Mickiewicz himself had a sad life, living during the era of Polish partition and suffering two periods of

Seasonal Celebrations

Special events: Krakow's main square is ideally suited to hosting family-friendly events all year round. Spacious, central, and atmospheric, the Rynek Główny comes into its own in the run-up to **Christmas,** when one of Europe's loveliest nativity scenes *(szopka)* is set up around the cobbled pavement. Stalls proffer gifts, sausages, and mulled wine, while a prize is given for the year's best *szopka*. After it closes, the main square prepares itself for the biggest celebration of the year, the **New Year's Eve** festivities—here's where Krakow's countdown takes place. Of the more unusual events at other times of the year, perhaps the most bizarre is September's **Dachshund Parade,** in which local sausage dogs are dressed in all manner of costumes and paraded from Barbikan to the main square down Floriańska. This whacky event is held in honor of local playwright Slawomir Mrożek, who demanded a parade of dachshunds be arranged to celebrate his homecoming in 1996. A prize is given to the best-looking dog.

exile, in Moscow and Paris. After his death in Istanbul, his body was brought to Wawel Cathedral (p 53, ❶) for burial. ⏱ *10 min. All trams to Old Town.*

Statue of Adam Mickiewicz.

❿ ★ **St. Adalbert's Church.** Surrounded by the pristine symmetry of the main market square, this, the oldest building on it, sticks out like a sore thumb. First, it is a complete jumble of styles, partly Romanesque, partly baroque, after various remakes in over a 1,000 years of service. During that time, the market square has been paved over and added to, leaving St. Adalbert's still set at its original level, at least 2m (6.5 ft.) lower than today's Rynek Główny. It's also tiny, the smallest church in Krakow, topped with a somewhat grandiose dome. Such a venerable anomaly is almost impossible to resist, although, once you're inside, the sundry collection of archaeological finds on display will merit just a quick perusal. ⏱ *30 min. Rynek Główny. ☎ 012/422-83-52. Free admission. Mon–Sat 9am–5pm, Sun 1:30–5pm. All trams to Old Town.*

Rynek Underground.

Modernist Krakow

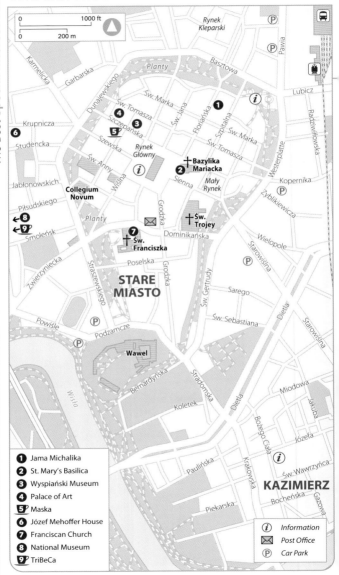

| 0 | | 1000 ft |
| 0 | 200 m | |

1 Jama Michalika
2 St. Mary's Basilica
3 Wyspiański Museum
4 Palace of Art
5 Maska
6 Józef Mehoffer House
7 Franciscan Church
8 National Museum
9 TriBeCa

i Information
✉ Post Office
Ⓟ Car Park

Modernism in Krakow developed when the city was granted a little autonomy from its Habsburg masters. This cultural phenomenon of the late 1800s to early 1900s involved a group of young artists known as Młoda Polska—"Young Poland." Including the key figures of Stanisław Wyspiański (1869–1907) and Józef Mehoffer (1869–1946), it was typified by striking colors and sinuous lines. START: **All trams to Old Town.**

① ★★ Jama Michalika. This historic coffeehouse not far from the main square was where the members of the Młoda Polska group would meet. In the back room, the seminal *Zielony Balonik* cabaret was staged, the puppets it featured still decoratively present amid the bright art of the Modernist movement. It still operates as a cafe-restaurant, albeit a tourist-friendly one, with a separate bar overlooking Floriańska at the front. ⏱ *30 min. Ul.Floriańska 45.* ☎ *012/422-15-61. Mon–Sat 9am–10pm. All trams to Old Town.*

② ★★ St. Mary's Basilica. Among the medieval treasures of this tourist jewel on the main square, you'll find quite stunning stained-glass designs and murals in the nave, created by Krakow's

most prominent Polish artists of the 19th century. ⏱ *20 min. See p 23,* **①**.

③ ★★★ Wyspiański Museum. Paintings, plans, designs, and models fill several small rooms here, demonstrating the range of work created by Stanisław Wyspiański, 19th-century architect, Art Nouveau artist, poet, and playwright. Self-portraits abound, plus studies of Wyspiański's Modernist contemporaries, including Józef Mehoffer in his studio. Theater sets and translated versions of Wyspiański's play *The Wedding* illustrate his literary output. Pride of place goes to a model of his revamped Wawel, *Acropolis*. Rooms look out onto an ivy-clad courtyard, decorated with a house-sized copy of one of the artist's friezes. ⏱ *1½ hr.*

Jama Michalika.

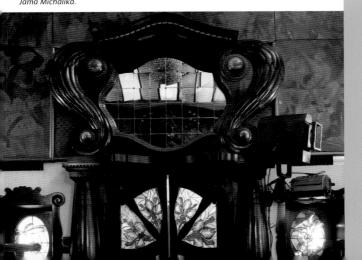

Palace of Art.

Ul.Szczepańska 11. ☎ 012/292-81-83. www.muzeum.krakow.pl. Admission 8 zł adults, 4 zł children. Free admission Sun. Wed–Sat 10am–6pm, Sun 10am–4pm. All trams to Old Town.

4 Palace of Art. Perhaps the definitive architectural statement of Modernism, the Secessionist Palace of Art was opened in 1901 and today belongs to the Friends of the Fine Arts organization. Busts of 19th-century Polish artists adorn Franciszek Mączyński's imaginative facade, designed to represent Doubt, Pain, and Despair, through which every artist must travel. You can make out Wyspiański and Matejko, among others. ⏱ *15 min. Pl.Szczepański 4. ☎ 012/422-66-16. Open hours vary according to exhibition. All trams to Old Town.*

5 Maska. The cafe of the Stary Theater round the corner from the Wyspiański Museum is an equal riot of Art Nouveau colors, keeping with the architectural style of the theater's facade. Both cafe and theater reflect the heyday of this venerable establishment, when the main personalities in Modernism would frequent it in the late 1800s. *Ul.Jagellońska 5. ☎ 012/422-85-66. zł.*

6 ★★ Józef Mehoffer House. Artist and designer Józef Mehoffer, a key member of the Młoda Polska artistic movement, bought this house in 1932. It belonged to the grandmother of his great contemporary, Stanisław Wyspiański, born under its roof in 1869. Walking through the various family rooms, their design and furnishings arranged by Mehoffer himself, you see how little has changed here—a room of 50 Japanese woodblock prints looks as it did in a 1938 photograph. The house was converted to a museum by Józef's son Zbigniew in 1969, on the centenary of his father's birth. The Café Ważka and pretty grounds are another delightful feature. ⏱ *40 min. Ul.Krupnicza 26. ☎ 012/370-81-86.*

Admission 6 zł adults, 3 zł children. Wed–Sat noon–6pm, Sun 10am–4pm. Free admission Sun. All trams to Teatr Bagatela.

7 ★ Franciscan Church.

Despite a history dating back more than 700 years, the Franciscan Church is best known for its Modernist masterpieces, namely the interior work of Stanisław Wyspiański. Light floods in through the Art Nouveau forms of his stained-glass creations on each of the north and south wings—flowers, stars, and swirling patterns against a blue background. Wyspiański was also responsible for the murals in the choir. *30 min. See p 14, 4.*

8 ★★★ National Museum.

Modern Polish art, decorative art, and military paraphernalia fill the rooms in this functional pre-war edifice situated by a major intersection west of the Old Town. You can buy a ticket for all floors, or just one for the 20th-century art separately.

There on the top floor, focus falls on the Młoda Polska and Grupa Krakowska movements, where works by Józef Mehoffer, Tadeusz Kantor, and Stanisław Wyspiański highlight their importance in the cultural life of the late 19th and early 20th centuries. *2 hr. Al.3 Maja 1. 012/295-56-00. www.muzeum.krakow.pl. Admission (combined) 18 zł adults, 9 zł children; Arms & Colors/Decorative Arts 10 zł adults, 5 zł children; 20th-Century Polish Art 10 zł adults, 5 zł children. Tues–Sat 10am–6pm, Sun 10am–4pm. Free admission Sun. All trams to Cracovia.*

9 TriBeCa.

In the lobby of the National Museum, this chic cafe is a cut above. Arabica coffee from Guatemala, *chocolatinis*, obscure fruit smoothies, focaccia sandwiches, toasts, and *tramezzini* all are served in stylish surroundings under a sea-scene ceiling. *Al.3 Maja 1. 012/633-53-31. zł.*

Młoda Polska Museum

Rydlówka: Those keen on learning more about Modernist Krakow, and happy to head out of the city center to do so, should head for Rydlówka. Here at **Ulica Tetmajera 28** (012/637-07-50), northwest of town in Bronowice Małe, is the peasant house where artist-dramatist Stanisław Wyspiański attended the wedding that inspired his play of the same name. This peasant house has since been converted into the **Młoda Polska Museum,** featuring art, poetry, costumes, and documentation from the Modernist period. The wedding in question took place in 1900. In 1968, a fire destroyed much of the house, which was converted into this museum a year later. It remains in the hands of the Rydlów family.

Krakow with Kids

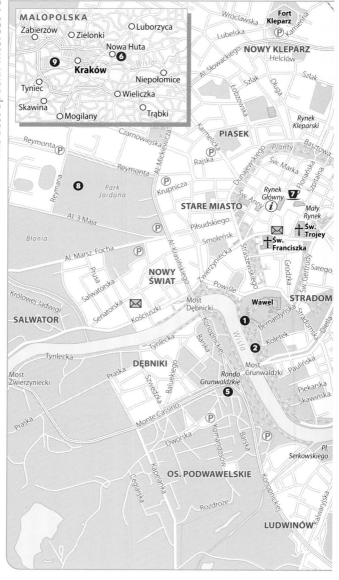

MALOPOLSKA

Zabierzów · Zielonki · Luborzyca · Nowa Huta **6** · **Kraków** **9** · Niepołomice · Tyniec · Wieliczka · Skawina · Mogilany · Trąbki

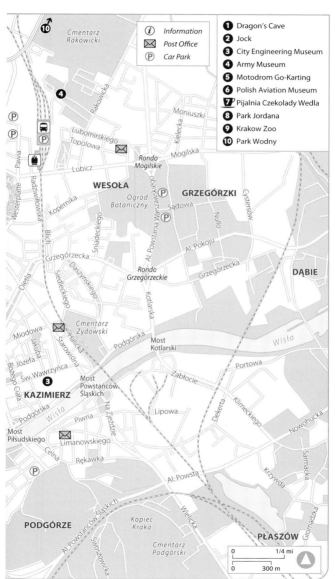

Legend

- ⓘ Information
- ✉ Post Office
- Ⓟ Car Park

1. Dragon's Cave
2. Jock
3. City Engineering Museum
4. Army Museum
5. Motodrom Go-Karting
6. Polish Aviation Museum
7. Pijalnia Czekolady Wedla
8. Park Jordana
9. Krakow Zoo
10. Park Wodny

Safe, compact, car-light, central Krakow is an easy city to get around. Nearly all bars, cafes, and restaurants—not to mention locals—are child-friendly, too. The couple of interactive museums, the zoo, the Aqua Park, and the main areas of green space are spread far apart, although city transport is good, cheap, and equally easy to negotiate. The cycle-friendly green ring of Planty (p 89) is another handy option for those confident on two wheels.
START: **All trams to Wawel.**

❶ ★★ **Dragon's Cave.** Having dragged the kids round the seemingly endless historic rooms of **Wawel Castle** (p 54, ❹), the least you can do is treat them to a big thrill at the bottom of the Dragon's Cave. Linked to the legend of the dragon who resided here before being tricked into defeat by a wily local cobbler, the summer-only cave involves a downward hike through tunnels, chambers, and corridors before you hit street level—and Bronisław Chromy's dragon statue scaring the pants off 4-year-olds with its regular fire-breathing antics. 🕐 *20 min. www.wawel-krakow.pl. Admission 3 zł. Daily Apr, Sept–Oct 10am–5pm; May–June 10am–6pm; July–Aug 10am–7pm. All trams to Wawel.*

Boating lake at Park Jordana.

❷ ★ **Jock.** A sad story, this, so break it to them gently. Canine Jock ("Dżok") sat at this spot for months, near the Grunwald Roundabout, where his master had died of a heart attack in his car. Later befriended and fed by an old local, he was taken to the dog pound after her death, only to escape to seek his favorite spot again. Haring back to the waterfront site, Jock was hit by a train and killed. Heartbroken local dog lovers clubbed together to commission this statue, another Chromy creation. 🕐 *10 min. Bulwar Czerwieński. Trams 18, 19, 22: Orzeszkowej.*

❸ ★★ **City Engineering Museum.** It's well worth your beating a path through deepest Kazimierz to reach this rare interactive museum, spread out around an old tram depot. First make a beeline for the **Fun and Science** section, where feats of engineering are explained by letting kids build their own bridges, pull levers, and generally make things sparkle, crackle, and bubble. The transportation section houses old trams and classic Polish-made cars through the ages. 🕐 *1 hr. Ul.Św.Wawrzyńca 15. ☎ 012/421-12-42. www.mimk.com.pl. Admission 8 zł adults, 5.50 zł children. Daily June–Sept 10am–6pm; Oct–May 10am–4pm. Trams 9, 13, 24, 34: Wawrzyńca.*

❹ **Army Museum.** Surrounded by abandoned buildings, Krakow's main military museum is currently undergoing a much-needed overhaul, but once open should contain enough displays to stir the imagination of youngsters with a passing interest in history. Displays focus on the Warsaw Uprising, and Polish struggles of the 1930s and 1940s. Maps, medals, newspapers, Gatling guns, and sundry equipment tell of the campaigns for Polish independence—so many with fatal consequences. ⏱ *30 min. Ul.Wita Stwosza 12.* ☎ *012/430-33-73. www.muzeum-ak.krakow.pl. All trams to Dworzec Główny.*

⑤ ★★ Motodrom Go-Karting. Moving from its Kazimierz base, the popular Motodrom has set up in the grounds of the disused behemoth Hotel Forum just over the river. Kids from 7 years old and up can whiz go-karts around the tire-lined course, Grand Prix flags and all. ⏱ *30 min. Ul.Konopnickiej.* ☎ *050-274-608. www.gokartymotodrom. yoyo.pl. Charge per 8 min 35 zł, 30 min 50 zł. Daily noon–10pm. Trams 18, 19, 22: Most Grunwaldzki. All buses to Rondo Grunwaldzkie.*

⑥ ★★★ Polish Aviation Museum. Set quite a way out of town toward Nowa Huta, this excellent attraction makes great use of its Rakowice airfield site. Soviet fighter jets line up outside, while displays within include one of Blériot's planes from 1909, and cover Polish flight from its very beginnings. It's all very hands-on, with plenty of interactive stuff for kids, as well as a cinema and library. ⏱ *1½ hr. Al. Jana Pawla II 17.* ☎ *012/640-99-60. www. muzeumlotnictwa.pl. Admission 10 zł adults, 5 zł children. Free admission Tues (outdoor exhibition only). Tues–Sun 9am–7pm. Trams 4, 5, 9, 10, 15, 40; buses 124, 424: AWF.*

⑦ ★ Pijalnia Czekolady Wedla. Wherever you're heading to or arriving from, you'll invariably pass this temple to chocolate and confectionery. Its grand surroundings befit a family tradition dating back 157 years. Enjoy a sumptuous hot chocolate on a winter's afternoon while the kids get messy. *Rynek Główny 46.* ☎ *012/429-40-85. złzł.*

⑧ ★ Park Jordana. Krakow's main recreational park lies just west of the outer ring road, a short distance from the city center. A fully equipped skate park complements the basketball and volleyball courts, slides, climbing frames, and a lake for paddleboats. ⏱ *2 hr. Aleja 3 Maja. Daily Apr–Oct 6am–10pm; Nov–Mar 6am–8pm. Trams 15, 18: Park Jordana n/z.*

⑨ ★★ Krakow Zoo. Set in the middle of Las Wolski woods (p 94), at the terminus of the 134 bus route from the Hotel Cracovia, Krakow's zoo has been in business for the best part of a century. Its global reputation as a breeding zoo is well earned—snow leopards to lynxes have all been raised here in captivity. Local species get a good look-in: Boar, bison, and the like. Mammals are given reasonable space—although some suffer from the bitter Polish winter. ⏱ *2 hr. See p 94,* ②.

⑩ ★★★ Park Wodny. Well worth the trek 5km (3 miles) northeast of town, Krakow's water park is superbly equipped, able to deliver a whole afternoon of fun. Pipes and slides include the world's longest shute, nearly 100m (328 ft.) of twists and turns for those 12 and above; a climbing wall; a paddling pool with a fairytale castle for toddlers; eight Jacuzzis; plus a lane pool and sauna for the grownups. ⏱ *2 hr. Ul.Dobrego Pasterza 126.* ☎ *012/616-31-90. www. parkwodny.pl. Admission 11 zł–22 zł adults; 42 zł–81 zł family. Daily 8am–10pm. All buses to Dobrego Pasterza.*

Jewish Krakow

1. Remuh Synagogue & Cemetery
2. Tall Synagogue
3. Old Synagogue
4. Popper Synagogue
5. Dawno temu na Kazimierzu
6. Galicia Jewish Museum
7. New Jewish Cemetery
8. Remnants of the Ghetto Wall
9. Plac Bohaterów Getta
10. Pharmacy Under the Eagle
11. Schindler's Factory

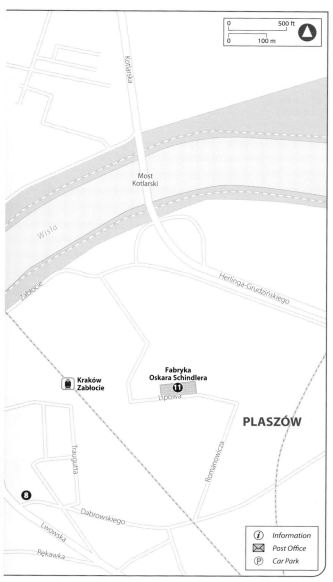

0 — 500 ft
0 — 100 m

Kotlarska

Most
Kotlarski

Wisła

Zabłocie

Herlinga-Grudzińskiego

**Kraków
Zabłocie**

**Fabryka
Oskara Schindlera**
11

Lipowa

PLASZÓW

Traugutta

Romanowicza

8

Dabrowskiego

Lwowska

Rękawka

i	Information
✉	Post Office
Ⓟ	Car Park

Krakow's Jews have been settled in Kazimierz since the end of the 14th century. The Nazi invasion saw Jews forced into a ghetto across the river in Podgórze, the site of horrendous atrocities. After decades of neglect, the recent renovation of Kazimierz's synagogues and revival of Jewish culture is a much welcomed phenomenon, and have helped make this the most vibrant district in the city. START: Trams 9, 13, 24, 34 to Miodowa.

1 ★★ **Remuh Synagogue & Cemetery.** It is apt that any tour of Jewish Krakow should start here, for the Remuh is its spiritual heart. Founded in 1553, the Remuh was known as the "New" Synagogue as it followed the "Old" one nearby. It was named after Moses Isserles (1520–72), or "Remuh," son of the founder and Chief Rabbi of Krakow in the 1500s. Its appearance changed with renovations in 1829 and 1933, and with the Nazi destruction soon after. Much of the modest interior—the bimah platform, the wall tablets—were rebuilt after the war. The Remuh is still a working house of prayer. Thousands of Jews from around the world flock to the rambling Remuh Cemetery, the gateway to your left as you leave the synagogue. Containing some of the oldest Jewish tombs in Poland, the cemetery was battered and used as

a rubbish tip by the Nazis—most of today's stones were excavated after the war. Pebbles are left on top as a mark of respect. Broken fragments were used to make a Wailing Wall to the right as you enter the hallowed ground. Sadly much of the far area flanked by Miodowa and Jakuba is still unkempt and shabby. ⏱ *1 hr. Szeroka 40.* ☎ *012/429-57-35. Admission 5 zł adults, 2 zł children. Sun–Thurs 9am–4pm, Fri 9am–3pm. Trams 9, 13, 24, 34: Miodowa.*

2 **Tall Synagogue.** A sharp turn right onto Józefa at the other end of Szeroka takes you to what is known as the Tall Synagogue. Named 'Tall' as its prayer rooms were above a row of shops supported by four buttresses, this was the third synagogue to open in Krakow. The bulk of its murals and furnishings did not survive World War II, but gradual

Remuh Cemetery, founded in 1553.

The Old Synagogue houses a museum of Judaism.

restoration has seen the Wysoka slowly come back to life. It currently houses an exhibition relating to a well-known Yiddish production by famed director Andrzej Wajda (b. 1926)—a theater was set up next door in the 1960s. The most prominent other feature here is the 17th-century portal on the opposite side of the otherwise bare main room. ⏲ *15 min. Józefa 38.* ☎ *012/426-75-20. Admission 10 zł adults, 7 zł children. Summer Sun–Fri 9am–7pm. Winter Sun–Fri 9am–5pm. Trams 9, 13, 24, 34: Miodowa.*

❸ ★★ Old Synagogue. Poland's oldest-surviving synagogue, and historic seat of the local Jewish authorities, this large, redbrick building was converted to a Museum of Judaism after its wartime destruction. Founded in the early 1400s—no one knows exactly when—the synagogue was rebuilt with Renaissance touches in 1570 after one of several fires, and added to over the centuries. Displays in the permanent exhibition cover local Jewish life and culture—shawls, yarmulke caps, and various ceremonial items are well presented and explained in English. Particular accent is placed on education—the layman gets a good idea of what it was like to grow up in this community a century ago. The striking bimah

platform is a reconstruction—the original staged many historic speeches, including one by Polish national hero Tadeusz Kościuszko (1746–1817) in 1794 urging Jews to join the Uprising. Upstairs is a display of documentation relating to the Nazi occupation. ⏲ *1 hr. Szeroka 24.* ☎ *012/422-09-62. www. mhk.pl. Admission 8 zł adults, 6 zł children. Mon 10am–2pm, Wed–Thurs, Sat–Sun 9am–4pm; Fri 10am–5pm. Last entry 30 min before closing. Trams 3, 9, 11, 13, 24: Wawrzyńca.*

❹ Popper Synagogue. Today an arts studio used by local children, the Popper Synagogue is part of the rich oral history of Jewish Kazimierz. It was named after Wolf Popper, a financier of the early 1600s, nicknamed "the Stork" after his habit of standing on one leg while addressing people. This was Krakow's most lavish synagogue, until its inevitable destruction at the hands of the Nazis. Its modern-day use lends it a colorful, lively atmosphere—bright banners usually decorate the inner courtyard as you walk through the main entrance between a stretch of landmark restaurants on focal Szeroka. ⏲ *15 min. Szeroka 16.* ☎ *012/ 421-29-87. Free admission. Trams 9, 13, 24, 34: Miodowa.*

5 Dawno temu na Kazimierzu.
"Once Upon a Time in Kazimierz" is both a historic reconstruction of the shops and workshops that thrived in this building before the war and a comfortable spot to tuck into specialties such as onion soup with caramel, duck fillet in cranberry sauce, or a stiff glass of Kosher vodka. *Szeroka 1.* ☎ *012/421-21-17. zł.*

6 ★★ Galicia Jewish Museum.
British photojournalist Chris Schwarz (1948–2007) is behind this thought-provoking exhibition, set in a converted warehouse. Aiming to broaden people's attention from the empty synagogues of Kazimierz and the death factory of Auschwitz, Schwarz and writer-historian Jonathan Webber set off around southern Poland (Galicia) to record the lesser-known places of murder and massacre—a plaque in a forest clearing or a ramshackle synagogue in some forgotten village. The result, intelligently themed and starkly displayed, offers some idea of the breadth and banality of the war crime. A bookstore, cafe, and information point provide further reason to visit. ⏱ *30 min. Dajwór 18.* ☎ *012/421-68-42. www.galiciajewishmuseum.org.*

Admission 15 zł adults, 8 zł children. Daily 10am–6pm. Trams 3, 9, 11, 13, 24: Wawrzyńca.

7 ★★ New Jewish Cemetery.
Over Starowiślna and under the railway viaduct on Miodowa stands the gateway to Krakow's largest Jewish cemetery, which opened as the Remuh closed in the early 1800s. As such, it houses some of the most prominent figures of Jewish life before World War II—poets, politicians, photographers—but the post-war renovation of this huge, overgrown site is still a long way from completion. It is still a working place of burial; new tombs are found close to the railway line. By the entrance stands a monument to Jews murdered during the war, built with broken tombstones, a sharp and striking reminder of how the cemetery must have looked when discovered in 1945. ⏱ *45 min. Miodowa 55. Mon–Thurs, Sun 9am–4pm; Fri 9am–3pm. Trams 3, 9, 11, 13, 24: Miodowa.*

8 ★ Remnants of the Ghetto Wall. Of the original wall created in March 1941 to pen in Krakow's Jews, only two fragments remain. On this one on Lwowska, a plaque in Polish and Hebrew speaks of their

The monument by the entrance of the New Jewish Cemetery.

Plac Bohaterów Getta.

suffering. The top of the wall was created in a running, half-moon pattern—an easily identifiable visual association with the shape of traditional Jewish gravestones. It's not much to see but what there is gives a clear idea of how the neighborhood was brutally divided during the Nazi occupation. 🕐 *10 min. Lwowska 25–29. Trams 9, 13, 24, 34: Pl.Bohaterów Getta.*

❾ ★ Plac Bohaterów Getta. A gray square just over the river from Kazimierz, "Heroes of the Ghetto Square" was once Plac Zgody, at the northern edge of the wartime Jewish Ghetto. This was where Jews were rounded up before being sent to concentration camps, and the site of an appalling Nazi massacre in March 1943. Today it is dotted with 70 chairs, the contemporary installation by Piotr Lewicki and Kazimierz Łatak harking back to the time when Jews had to discard their furniture before being sent to their death. The focus on such everyday items brings home the evil of the heinous crimes committed here. Nowadays lined by new shops and businesses, the square features signposts and maps indicating the main sites of the Jewish Ghetto and, in one corner, the Pharmacy Under the Eagle museum.

🕐 *15 min. Trams 9, 13, 24, 34: Pl.Bohaterów Getta.*

❿ ★★ Pharmacy Under the Eagle. A place in history for this former working pharmacy is assured, thanks to the brave work of its owner, Tadeusz Pankiewicz. Converted to a museum in 1983, the Apteka Pod Orłem, the only pharmacy in the Jewish Ghetto set up by the Nazis in 1941 became a secret resource and meeting place for Jews attempting to survive the atrocities. Their activities, selflessly facilitated by Pankiewicz, are illustrated and documented here, in the form of film

Remnants of the Ghetto Wall.

Pharmacy Under the Eagle.

footage, original artifacts, and explanations in four languages. Particularly harrowing are the descriptions of people who sought escape through the sewers—others falling and drowning—to an uncertain fate at the other end. Note also the letters of gratitude sent by various Jewish organizations to Pankiewicz after the war. 🕐 *30 min. 18 Pl.Bohaterów*

Getta. ☎ *012/656-56-25. Admission 6 zł adults, 5 zł children. Free admission Mon. Apr–Oct Mon 10am–2pm, Tues–Sun 9:30am–5pm; Nov–Mar Mon 10am–2pm, Tues–Thurs, Sat 9am–4pm, Fri 10am–5pm. Closed first Tues of the month. Trams 9, 13, 24, 34: Pl.Bohaterów Getta.*

⓫ Schindler's Factory. After years of neglect and then renovation, the famous factory of Schindler lore has been converted into one of the city's most popular attractions. After walking through the main entrance under the sign *Fabryka Oskara Schindlera—Emaila,* you are immediately transported back into the Krakow of Oskar Schindler's day, the Krakow of the Nazi occupation and persecution of the Jews. You find yourself sitting in a Polish barber shop with dangerous gossip played over the speakers, or stooping into a bunker where a family would have lived for months. There's a room done up as the one used by factory boss Schindler, and a cafe themed after the film. 🕐 *1½ hr. Lipowa 4.* ☎ *012/57-10-17. Admission 15 zł adults, 13 zł children. Free admission Mon. Apr–Oct Mon 10am–4pm, Tues–Sun 10am–8pm; Nov–Mar Mon 10am–2pm, Tues–Sun 10am–6pm. Closed first Mon of the month. Trams 9, 13, 24, 34: Pl.Bohaterów Getta.* ●

Mind Your Head

Yarmulke: All male visitors to sacred Jewish sites must wear the yarmulke traditional skullcap as a sign of reverence. In Krakow, this is particularly required at the two main Jewish cemeteries. At the Remuh, a man will hand men a yarmulke (a Yiddish word possibly of Polish origin) from a bag of them at the door to the synagogue. At the New Cemetery, a girl might dash out from the funeral house by the gate and hand you one. If no yarmulke is immediately to hand, don't just breeze in regardless—a supply will be put out somewhere by the entrance.

Old **Town**

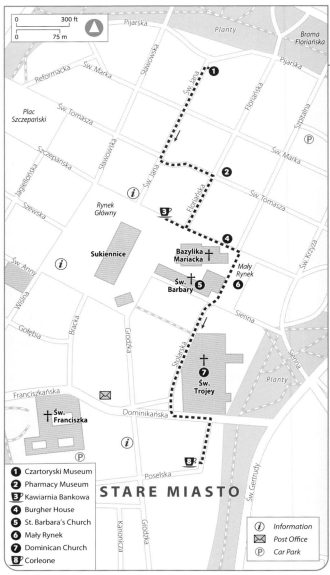

1 Czartoryski Museum
2 Pharmacy Museum
3 Kawiarnia Bankowa
4 Burgher House
5 St. Barbara's Church
6 Mały Rynek
7 Dominican Church
8 Corleone

(i) Information
✉ Post Office
Ⓟ Car Park

Previous page: Vis a Vis Café.

Krakow's Old Town offers relaxed tourism at its best. Easily walkable, with churches, shops, and museums at almost every turn, the streets of the Stare Miasto surrounding the main market square provide plenty to captivate the casual visitor. The grid pattern of well-signposted streets is easy to negotiate, so you may not even need a map. START: **All trams to Barbican.**

❶ ★★★ **Czartoryski Museum.** A cornucopia of random European treasures awaits at one of Krakow's most endearing museums. It contains one of only three Da Vinci oil paintings in the world, *Lady with an Ermine*; a Rembrandt landscape; assorted worthy Spanish, Venetian, and Flemish pieces, as well as some personal artifacts of Napoleon, Captain Cook, and Frederick the Great. A major renovation is set to run until 2012. ⏲ 1 ½ hr. *Św.Jana 19.* ☎ *012/422-55-66. www. muzeum-krakow.pl. Check opening times and prices on website.*

❷ ★ **kids** **Pharmacy Museum.** Often overlooked despite its central location, this quirky attraction is full of surprises. One of the most voluminous of its kind, the Pharmacy Museum fills five floors of a splendid 15th-century building, each done out to look like an apothecary from a particular century or, in the case of the basement and loft, an underground laboratory and herb-drying

room, respectively. Furniture, chests, cupboards, and vessels are original, many taken from monasteries across Poland. The result feels authentic and close to how people lived down the centuries. ⏲ 1 hr. *Floriańska 25.* ☎ *012/421-92-79, www.muzeumfarmacji.pl. Admission 9 zł adults, 6 zł children. Tues noon–6:30pm, Wed–Sun 10am–2:30pm.*

❸ **Kawiarnia Bankowa.** On the Floriańska corner of the main market square, this terrace cafe is a handy pit stop for those exploring the northeast side of the Old Town. Renovated in 1998, with an interior dating back to World War I, the Bankowa offers breakfasts and snacks along with the usual range of coffees and drinks. *Rynek Główny 47.* ☎ *012/429-56-77. złzł.*

❹ ★ **kids** **Burgher House.** The Hippolits family lived in this grand

Czartoryski Museum.

Burgher House, once home to the Hippolits family.

time—the grandfather clock and bed-warmer in the bedroom, the keyboard in the music room, the visiting cards in the hallway. Documentation is in the form of laminated cards in English and Polish. So close to the main square you can hear the bugle player on the hour from St. Mary's, the Burgher House provides a quiet and welcome distraction from the daily life of 21st-century Krakow. ⊕ *45 min. Pl.Mariacki 3.* ☎ *012/422-42-19. www.mhk.pl. Admission 7 zł adults, 5 zł children. Free admission Wed. May–Oct Wed–Sun 10am–5:30pm; Nov–Apr Wed, Fri–Sun 9am–4pm, Thurs noon–7pm. Closed 2nd Sun of the month.*

town house at the turn of the 17th century. The house, somewhat older, has been converted into a museum to illustrate the lives and pleasures of those who lived in Krakow at the time. Up a shiny wooden staircase, you are led through a series of rooms, each filled with furniture and objects relating to daily life at the

5 St. Barbara's Church. Generally only open for mass, St. Barbara's was built around the same time as St. Mary's diagonally opposite, reputedly with leftover bricks. Its facade is Gothic in appearance, with figures from the workshop of Veit Stoss (of St. Mary's altar fame) at the entrance. Worth a quiet stroll around the outside. ⊕ *10 min. Mały Rynek.* ☎ *012/428-15-00.*

St. Barbara's Church on Mały Rynek square.

People watch from a cafe on Mały Rynek.

6 ★ **Mały Rynek.** The smaller (but not younger) of the two adjoining market squares in the heart of Krakow feels calm after the tourist mayhem of Rynek Główny. The grand surrounds of symmetrical town houses and the sides of St. Mary's (p 23) and St. Barbara's churches lend the Mały Rynek a dignified atmosphere—best enjoyed from one of the cafe terraces. ⏱ *10 min.*

7 ★ **Dominican Church.** Standing at the gateway to the cluster of churches set between the main market square and Wawel, the Dominican Church is a late 19th-century rebuild of the 13th-century Gothic original. Many of the ornate chapels survived, most notably the Myszkowski, with busts of the family lining the dome. ⏱ *30 min. Stolarska 12.* ☎ *012/423-16-13. Daily 8am–8pm.*

8 **Corleone.** A standard but reliable Italian eatery, happy to provide tasty favorites to weary sightseers at the end of a hard morning's work. Corleone currently offers lunchtime specials on weekdays—risotto is the recommended choice. There is an excellent selection of wines, too, augmented by Tuscan labels, a feature of Thursday wine-and-music evenings. *Poselska 19.* ☎ *012/429-51-26. www.corleone.krakow.pl. zł zł.*

Princess Izabela Czartoryska

Founder of Poland's first-ever museum, Princess Izabela Czartoryska was a major socialite and art collector of the late 1700s and early 1800s. Becoming a princess by dint of her marriage to Prince Adam Kazimierz Czartoryski in 1761, the former Countess Fleming was influenced by her sojourn in Paris a decade later. There she met Benjamin Franklin, Voltaire, and Jean-Jacques Rousseau, returning to Poland to convert the Czartoryski Palace into a center for intellectual debate and discussion. Following its destruction during the Uprising against Russia, she had it rebuilt and filled with rare treasures. It was her grandson, Wladyslaw, who had it converted in 1878 into the Czartoryski Museum (p 45, **1**) we know today.

University Quarter

1. Wyspiański Museum
2. Palace of Art
3. St. Anne's Church
4. Collegium Maius
5. Café U Pęcherza
6. Statue of Nicolaus Copernicus
7. Capuchin Church
8. Carmelite Church
9. Museum of Insurance
10. Museum Emeryka Hutten-Czapskiego

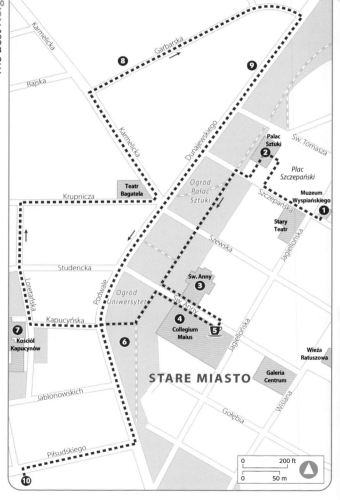

The venerable buildings of the Jagiellonian University dot cobbled streets, creating a tranquil, erudite atmosphere. The oldest, geared to tourists, is the Collegium Maius, where Krakow's most celebrated pupil, Nicolaus Copernicus (1473–1543), studied in the 1490s. Some 45,000 students enroll at 15 faculties—the University Quarter is as vibrant now as it was 500 years ago. START: **All trams to Teatr Bagatela.**

❶ ★★★ Wyspiański Museum. The life and achievements of Stanisław Wyspiański, 19th-century architect, Art Nouveau artist, poet, and playwright are celebrated at this renovated attraction. His paintings, plans, designs, and models fill several small rooms—you'll find yourself overwhelmed at the range of work. 🕐 *1 hr. See p 29,* ❸.

❷ Palace of Art. Although the exhibition program here is varied and may not feature the kind of art you're into, the building alone is worth the detour. Created in Secessionist style in 1901, it belongs to the Friends of the Fine Arts organization. Busts of 19th-century Polish artists adorn Franciszek Mączyński's imaginative facade, designed to represent Doubt, Pain, and Despair, through which every artist must

Wyspiański Museum—home of artist, poet, and playwright.

St. Anne's, also known as the University Church.

travel. You can make out Wyspiański and Matejko, among others. 🕐 *15 min. See p 30,* ❹.

❸ St. Anne's Church. Also known as the University Church—famous students and professors are represented, including Copernicus—baroque St. Anne's was Gothic but rebuilt in sumptuous style by Tylman van Gameren (1632–1706) in the late 1600s. The plasterwork and altars were the work of Baltasare Fontana—as you walk around the airy nave, it's hard to tell which pillars are real and which painted. To the right of the main entrance stands the shrine of St. John of Kęty, also by Fontana, the remains of the former professor held up by figures representing four University faculties.

⏲ 15 min. Św.Anny 11. ☎ 012/422-53-18. Daily 9am–noon, 4–7pm.

④ ★★★ kids Collegium Maius. Accessed by tour only—book your place on the next English-language one taking place that day—the University Museum contains remarkable treasures whose significance is entertainingly described by your guide. The 30 minutes fly by as you are shown lecture rooms and ceremonial halls, taking in a copper globe from the early 1500s with the Americas depicted for the first time, an astrolabe from Arabia dated 1054, and astronomical instruments from when Copernicus studied here in the 1490s. In the cramped **Copernicus Room,** your guide will point out discs, globes, and instruments he would have used. Sadly, much of the paperwork is facsimile—the Swedes took the original Copernicus collection, kept today at the Uppsala University Library. Your visit culminates with the ornate Aula where graduation ceremonies still take place. Text over its Renaissance portal reads: *Plus Ratio Quam Vis*—"Let Reason Prevail Over Strength." A further hour-long tour takes in the permanent art collection (with pieces by Rembrandt and Rubens). A child-friendly interactive exhibition runs on occasional mornings. ⏲ *40 min. Ul.Jagiellońska 15. ☎ 012/422-05-49. www.maius.uj.edu.pl. Admission (by tour only) 12 zł adults, 6 zł children. Apr–Oct Mon, Wed, Fri 10am–2:20pm, Tues, Thurs 10am–5:20pm, Sat 10am–2:40pm; Nov–Mar Mon, Wed–Fri 10am–2:20pm, Tues 10am–3:20pm, Sat 10am–2:40pm.*

5 Café U Pęcherza. In the basement of the Collegium Maius, this labyrinthine cafe displays the Kashary archaeological dig near Odessa. Students chat casually over coffee, cakes, and snacks beneath pictures of their professors unearthing Greek treasures. *Ul.Jagiellońska 15. ☎ 012/422-05-49. zł.*

⑥ Statue of Nicolaus Copernicus. Outside the Collegium Novum on the edge of the Planty, Krakow's most famous student is in a reflective mood, a primitive astronomical instrument to hand. The plinth refers to his year of study here being 1491. Behind stands the main University building, where concerts are given in the **Aula Magna** lecture hall. A plaque marks the professors sent to concentration camps in 1939. ⏲ *10 min.*

⑦ kids Capuchin Church. The church of the Capuchin friars reflects the simplicity of their Order—the real architectural treasure here is the **Loreto Chapel,** built outside in the early 1700s, 2 decades after the friars first arrived. Connected to the church by cloister, the chapel makes this brief diversion worthwhile with its statue of the Madonna set within a striking altar.

Café U Pęcherza.

At Christmas, a mechanical nativity scene uses characters from Polish history and folklore. 🕐 *20 min. Loretańska 11.* ☎ *012/422-48-03. Daily 9:30am–7pm. All trams to Teatr Bagatela.*

⑧ ★ Carmelite Church.

There's a patchwork history to this votive church, also known as the Church on the Sand. Legend has it that this was the spot where the 11th-century Duke of Poland, Władysław Herman, discovered a pile of sand used to heal a terrible pox on his legs. Destroyed by the Swedes, this church was rebuilt in baroque style in the 17th century. An icon of the **Madonna of the Sand** covers one wall. Note the two-room sacristy, renovated to its former glory, altar, cabinets, chandelier and all. 🕐 *30 min. Karmelicka 19.* ☎ *012/632-67-52. Daily 9:30am–4:30pm, 5–7pm. All trams to Teatr Bagatela.*

⑨ Museum of Insurance.

The only one of its kind in the world, the Museum of Insurance was set up in 1987 on the 175th anniversary of Polish insurance companies. Covering 200 years of this seemingly prosaic trade, it shows the breadth and history of the insurance business by means of thousands of documents, photographs, and tools. 🕐 *30 min. Dunajewskiego 3.* ☎ *012/422-82-11. Free admission. Tues–Fri 9–11am. All trams to Teatr Bagatela.*

Statue of Nicolaus Copernicus.

⑩ Museum Emeryka Hutten-Czapskiego.

This branch of the National Museum (p 31, ⑧) is closed for renovation until 2012. When it reopens, it will be home to a comprehensive collection of Polish coins, medals, and banknotes, much of which the 19th-century collector Emeryk Hutten-Czapski gathered in his lifetime. 🕐 *30 min. Piłsudskiego 12.* ☎ *012/625-73-10. www.muzeum.krakow.pl. Check website for up-to-date opening hours and admission. All trams to Teatr Bagatela.*

The church of the Capuchin friars.

Wawel

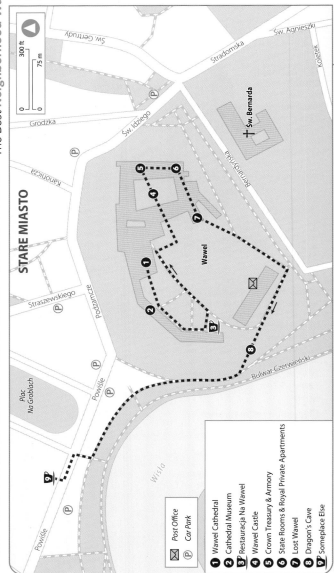

300 ft
75 m
0

Św. Gertrudy

Św. Agnieszki

Stradomska

Koletek

Grodzka

Św. Idziego

Św. Bernarda

STARE MIASTO

Kanonicza

Bernardyńska

Wawel

Straszewskiego

Podzamcze

Powiśle

Bulwar Czerwieński

Plac
Na Groblach

Powiśle

Wisła

Powiśle

⊠ Post Office

Ⓟ Car Park

1 Wawel Cathedral
2 Cathedral Museum
3 Restauracja Na Wawel
4 Wawel Castle
5 Crown Treasury & Armory
6 State Rooms & Royal Private Apartments
7 Lost Wawel
8 Dragon's Cave
9 Someplace Else

Wawel is Krakow's Westminster Abbey, Notre-Dame, and Vatican. This is where Polish kings were crowned, where Polish monarchs, poets, and generals lie buried, and where trophies from historic Polish battles were presented. At the main gate, a digital ticker records sales of timed tickets up to the day's limit—be in line early and you'll get in. START: **All trams to Wawel.**

❶ ★★★ kids Wawel Cathedral.
Poland's most sacred building is a visual assault. Buying your ticket opposite the Cathedral, you enter the nave crammed with treasures and lined with bright chapels and ornate tombs. Following the arrows, your eye picks out the most striking elements: The **Zygmunt Chapel,** on the right-hand side, is the Renaissance at its most exquisite; in the middle, the tomb of King Jan III Sobieski (1629–96), hero of the Battle of Vienna, is baroque; and, near it, the tomb of King Jan Olbracht (1459–1501) is late Gothic. On the left-hand side is the entrance to the **Royal Crypt,** and farther along is the **Zygmunt Tower.** The former involves a shuffle around tombs grouped by dynasty, although those of military heroes and poets give

light relief. For the tower, climb the narrow, steep staircase for views of Krakow. The **Zygmunt Bell,** around 2m (6.5 ft.) in diameter, is only used for special occasions—reach up to touch the clapper with your left hand for luck. ⏱ *1½ hr. Wawel 3.* ☎ *697-73-68-63. www.katedra-wawelska.pl. Admission 12 zł adults, 7 zł children. Mon–Sat 9am–3:30pm, Sun 12:30–3:30pm. Last entry 30 min before closing.*

❷ ★ Cathedral Museum. Turn immediately right as you come out of the Cathedral and you arrive at a modest building and a small, square front garden. This is the Cathedral Museum, opened by Archbishop Karl Wojtyła (1920–2005) in 1978 before becoming Pope John Paul II. Over two floors, you'll find robes

Poland's most sacred building—Wawel Cathedral.

and regalia of sundry Polish kings—the brightest being the coronation robe of Stanisław August Poniatowski (1732–98), dated 1764—and oddities such as four slabs from the 10th-century St. Gereon's Church. Much of the top floor is given over to paraphernalia pertaining to John Paul II, either as Pope or as Archbishop of Krakow. ⏱ *40 min. Wawel 3.* ☎ *012/429-33-27. www.katedra-wawelska.pl. Admission included with Wawel Cathedral ticket. Mon–Sat 9am–4pm.*

3 **Restauracja Na Wawel.** The only full-blown restaurant in the Wawel complex, this one offers hefty meat dishes with all the trimmings, along with fish options, soups, and a good selection of blini. Not cheap, but the expansive terrace looking over Krakow more than compensates. There's a separate, cheaper snack bar. *Wzgórze Wawelskie 9.* ☎ *012/421-19-15. złzł.*

Wawel Castle.

4 ★★★ **kids** **Wawel Castle.** A short walk from the Cathedral leads to an arcaded Renaissance courtyard, surrounded on three sides by a fine Italianate building crammed with historic goodies. Modest lines form by the doorways of two main museums: The State Rooms and Royal Private Apartments, and the Crown Treasury and Armory, both requiring tickets from the main kiosk. Round the corner, within the outer courtyard gardens centerpiecing the Wawel complex, is the Lost Wawel exhibition. The people making strange movements in the northwest corner of the inner courtyard are reacting to the energy said to resonate from the black stone of the former **St. Gereon's Church** behind the wall. ⏱ *1½ hr. Wawel Hill.* ☎ *012/422-51-55 (ext 219). www.wawel-krakow.pl. Daily 6am–dusk.*

5 ★ **kids** **Crown Treasury & Armory.** The lesser of the two inner courtyard museums will impress the boys with its many swords, cannons, crossbows, muskets, and spiky things on chains. As for the Treasury, the assortment of medals, coins, and goblets includes an 11th-century chalice belonging to the Tyniec abbots. ⏱ *40 min. Admission 15 zł adults, 8 zł children. Free admission Sun. Tues–Sun 9:30am–4pm.*

6 ★★ **kids** **State Rooms & Royal Private Apartments.** Here, top-floor State Rooms involve a lengthy but enjoyable walk through numerous interconnecting doorways, leading to elaborately decorated spaces. Look out for the Hans Dürer scenes in the **Tournament Room** and Flemish tapestries in the Planet, Eagle, and Envoys' rooms, where 30 carved heads on the ceiling are what the kids will be raving about. You access the Royal Private Apartments by guided tour,

The Renaissance courtyard at Wawel Castle.

hence the higher ticket price—but the Flemish tapestries, Meissen porcelain, and rich furnishings make it worthwhile. Don't miss the 14th-century Gothic Hen's Foot tower, Renaissance paintings, a fireplace from 1600, and the view of Krakow from the windows. ⏱ *40 min. Admission 15 zł–20 zł adults, 8 zł children. State Rooms Tues–Sat 9:30am–4pm, Sun 10am–4pm. Apartments Tues–Sat 9:30am–4pm.*

7 ★★ **kids Lost Wawel.** A millennium of finds from Wawel Hill are displayed around a descending series of spiral walkways—visitors stop to gawp at kitchenware, leather shoes, and paving tiles used here down the centuries. The foundations of the 10th-century Rotunda that once stood here, and models of St. Gerleon's Church and Wawel in its various stages, also draw interest. A film show of historic treasures plays by the entrance. ⏱ *40 min.*

Admission 7 zł adults, 4 zł children. Tues–Sat 9:30am–4pm, Sun 10am–4pm.

8 ★★ **kids Dragon's Cave.** Every kid's favorite attraction at Wawel. Linked with the legend of a dragon overcome by a wily shoemaker, this summer-only amusement takes you along tunnels, chambers, and corridors until you arrive at the Vistula embankment—and Bronisław Chromy's dragon statue breathing out great sparks of fire. ⏱ *20 min. See p 34,* **1**.

9 **Someplace Else.** The Sheraton Hotel's terrace sports bar, near the exit of the Dragon's Cave, offers the family easy Tex-Mex choices from noon onwards. Live music makes a longer stay worthwhile for the grownups. *Powiśle 7.* ☎ *012/ 662-16-70. złzłzł.*

Kazimierz

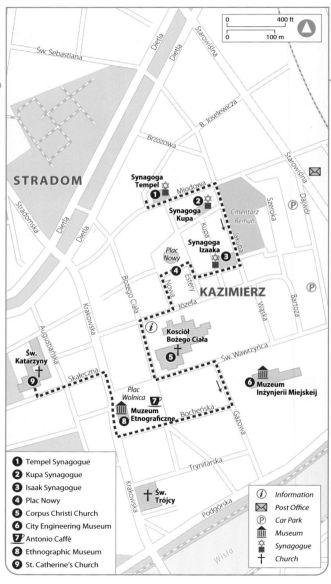

1 Tempel Synagogue
2 Kupa Synagogue
3 Isaak Synagogue
4 Plac Nowy
5 Corpus Christi Church
6 City Engineering Museum
7 Antonio Caffè
8 Ethnographic Museum
9 St. Catherine's Church

ⓘ Information
✉ Post Office
Ⓟ Car Park
🏛 Museum
✡ Synagogue
✝ Church

Kazimierz has re-emerged from the remnants of World War II. This former Jewish quarter contains Krakow's busiest bar hub, contemporary restaurants, and a mall with a multiplex. The long-dormant Jewish culture is vibrant again, with a major annual festival. The Christian churches and museums clustered in this compact district echo Kazimierz's historic and multicultural past. **START: All trams to Dietla/Krakowska.**

❶ ★★ Tempel Synagogue. Of Kazimierz's half-dozen synagogues, the first you find as you cross over at the Dietla/Krakowska crossroads is perhaps the most attractive—and controversial. Built outside the original 17th-century ghetto walls, the Tempel was also known as the Progressive Synagogue for the inclusive nature of its services. Built in the 1860s by Jews who had been assimilated into the local culture, the Tempel features three dozen stained-glass windows, with inscriptions in Polish and Hebrew—traditionalists were horrified! Today the Tempel is best visited during one of its regular chamber concerts. It also hosts the opening of June's Jewish Culture Festival (p 164). *20 min. Miodowa 24.* 📞 *012/429-57-35. Admission 5 zł adults, 2 zł children. Sun–Thurs 10am–4pm, Fri 9am–3pm.*

❷ ★ Kupa Synagogue. The recent substantial renovation of this 350-year-old synagogue comes after 5 decades of neglect. Biblical scenes and images of Israel now embellish the ceiling; signs of the Zodiac in the women's gallery and the depictions of Noah backdrop concerts and exhibitions regularly held here. General admission is free, making the Kupa a pleasant and easy diversion on any local wander. *15 min. Miodowa 27. Free admission. Mon–Fri, Sun 9am–6pm.*

❸ ★ Isaak Synagogue. The biggest of Kazimierz's synagogues has also benefited from recent major renovation. The 17th- and 18th-century murals are now restored and visitors are greeted with a video loop of original newsreel films shot around Kazimierz in less peaceful times, one of general street life in

Tempel, also known as the Progressive Synagogue.

Kupa Synagogue.

the 1930s, the other of Nazi round-ups. ⏱ *20 min. Kupa 18.* ☎ *012/430-22-22. Admission 5 zł adults, 3 zł children. Mon–Thurs, Sun 9am–4pm, Fri 9am–1pm.*

❹ ★ **Plac Nowy.** The square at the heart of Kazimierz sums up its history and contemporary revival perfectly. Known by locals as Jewish Square, "New Square" is center-pieced by a round market building which Jews used as a poultry slaughterhouse before the war. Now it is ringed by little hatches serving toasted sandwiches in long, half-baguette form, wielded by bar-hoppers as they flit from venue to venue around the cafe-choked square. Plac Nowy still operates as a market: Produce in the week and second-hand clothes on Sundays.

❺ ★★ **Corpus Christi Church.** As you walk south from Plac Nowy, you are entering the old Christian part. The church founded by Kazimierz the Great (1310–70) in the 1300s is a mixture of styles reflecting its patchwork history, its tower rising 70m (230 ft.) over the skyline. Raided by Swedish, Russian, and Austrian troops, Corpus Christi offers unusual but worthy features in various architectural styles. Walking round the spacious grounds, used as a graveyard in the 16th century, you come across a roofed, caged-in model of *Christ in the Garden of Gethsemane*, an image that stays with you as you enter the

Corpus Christi Church, founded by Kazimierz the Great.

Gothic portal. Features of the three-aisled interior include a boat-shaped pulpit, mermaids, oars, fishing nets, and, in the north aisle, the tomb of Florentine architect Bartolomeo Berecci (1480–1537). Responsible for many of Wawel's Renaissance touches, Berecci died in odd circumstances in the market square in 1537. ⏱ *20 min. Bożego Ciała 25.* ☎ *012/ 430-62-90. Mon–Sat 8:30am–noon, 1–7pm, Sun (not during mass) 6:30am–8pm.*

6 ★★ kids City Engineering Museum.

More entertaining than its name suggests, this museum set in a former tram depot should keep most kids occupied for an hour or so. Few museums in town offer a hands-on approach, so the Fun and Science section's interactive take on science and engineering is welcome. The transportation section concentrates on Polish models, such as a Polski Fiat car from 1936, weird post-war prototypes (look out for the back-to-front one from 1957), and classic local makes from the 1960s. ⏱ *1 hr. See p 34,* ❸.

7 Antonio Caffè.

An easy and pleasant option on a main square, this shiny red cafe offers Italian standards, cakes, sorbets, and quality appetizers. Chic decorative touches keep the clientele selective. *Wolnica 13.* ☎ *012/430-59-99. zł.*

8 ★★ kids Ethnographic Museum.

Set in Kazimierz Town Hall, a striking building dating back to the 1500s, the Ethnographic Museum is thorough, imaginative, and surprisingly entertaining. Starting through the main entrance with five life-size reproductions of peasant houses from specific villages in Poland—note the tiny beds, bizarre snowshoes, and cheese presses—the permanent exhibition moves upstairs to the extensive section concentrating on the life cycle in rural Poland in the 19th- and early 20th-centuries. Birth, toys, pastimes, school, farm life, work, military service, church, weddings, political life, institutions, newspapers, music, and family celebrations are exhaustively illustrated with a wealth of material (artifacts, film, interviews) with documentation also given in English. ⏱ *1 hr. Pl.Wolnica 1.* ☎ *012/ 430-60-23. www.mek.krakow.pl. Admission 9 zł adults, 5 zł children. Tues–Wed, Fri–Sat 11am–7pm, Thurs 11am–9pm, Sun 11am–3pm.*

9 ★ St. Catherine's Church.

One of Krakow's most beautiful Gothic churches stands on Kazimierz's far western edge, toward the river. Founded by Kazimierz the Great in the 1300s, it contains murals from that era, in the cloisters, but many of the other historic features within have been lost in earthquakes and invasions. Look out for the baroque altar and Gothic vestibule. ⏱ *30 min. Ul.Augustiańska 7.* ☎ *012/430-62-42. www.parafia-kazimierz.augustianie. pl. Open for mass only.*

Motorbikes at the City Engineering Museum.

Podgórze & Płaszów

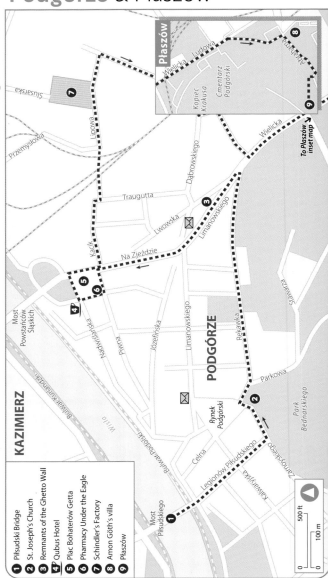

Płaszów

KAZIMIERZ

PODGÓRZE

Park Bednarskiego

To Płaszów inset map

1 Piłsudski Bridge
2 St. Joseph's Church
3 Remnants of the Ghetto Wall
4 Qubus Hotel
5 Plac Bohaterów Getta
6 Pharmacy Under the Eagle
7 Schindler's Factory
8 Amon Göth's villa
9 Płaszów

Immediately facing Kazimierz over the Vistula, Podgórze was the location of the wartime Jewish Ghetto. Although inevitably linked with the terrible events of the 1940s, Podgórze is enjoying a major revival. Bars and restaurants that would have comfortably rubbed shoulders with the fashionable spots of Kazimierz 5 years ago have been set up on this side of the river. START: **Trams 3, 6, 8, 10: Korona.**

1 Piłsudski Bridge. The most dramatic of the bridges over the Vistula was opened in 1933. Three cast-iron arches rise criss-crossed over the river, allowing views of historic Wawel and the new businesses of Podgórze on each side. Built to ease the pressure on the nearby Habsburg Podgórski Bridge, since demolished, the Piłsudski Bridge now seems in constant motion, the regular rattle of trams and traffic vibrating under the feet of pedestrians as they cross on the outer footpaths. The Podgórze side is ideal for a waterside stroll, back toward town. ⏱ *10 min.*

2 ★ St. Joseph's Church. Look toward Podgórze from anywhere in the city and this spire dominates the skyline—prolific church architect Jan Sas-Zubrzycki (1860–1935) was hoping to copy the landmark effect that the spire of St. Mary's has on the

main market square of the Old Town. Opened in 1909, when the Habsburgs still controlled this rival side of the river, the large neo-Gothic St. Joseph's Church towers over Podgórze's own main market square, but is somewhat underwhelming once you enter—take a walk around its recently renovated exterior for a better impression. ⏱ *20 min. Rynek Podgórski.*

3 ★ Remnants of the Ghetto Wall. Most tour buses that crawl through Podgórze make a stop at this otherwise nondescript stretch of sidewalk. Here stands one of two fragments of the original 3m (100-ft.) high wall created in March 1941 to pen in Krakow's Jews. A plaque in Polish and Hebrew speaks of their suffering. The top of the wall was created in a running, half-moon pattern—an easily identifiable visual association with the shape of

Piłsudski Bridge on the Vistula.

St Joseph's, built by prolific church architect Jan Sas-Zubrzycki.

traditional Jewish gravestones.
🕐 *10 min. See p 40,* **8**.

4 **Qubus Hotel.** If anything strikes the most contrast between the remnants of wartime tragedy and 21st-century Podgórze, it's this

Plac Bohaterów Getta.

glitzy business and leisure hotel, opened in 2006. Take a break from a morning on the Schindler trail with coffee, cakes, or open sandwiches at the Barracuda lobby bar. The **After Work** piano bar and **Mile Stone** jazz club provide swish drinks and entertainment for those arriving from early evening. *Nadwiślańka 6.* ☎ *012/374-51-00. złzłzł.*

5 ★ **Plac Bohaterów Getta.** "Heroes of the Ghetto" Square, formerly Plac Zgody, was the site of the regular round-ups and the Nazi massacre of Jews in March 1943. Its bloody legacy has been illustrated by means of 70 chairs, a contemporary installation by Piotr Lewicki and Kazimierz Łatak harking back to the time when Jews had to discard their furniture before being sent to the death camps. The facades of new shops and businesses do little to diminish your imagination as your eyes pass over the stark, open square. 🕐 *15 min. See p 41,* **9**.

6 ★★ **Pharmacy Under the Eagle.** Converted to a museum in 1983, Tadeusz Pankiewicz's original pharmacy was a resource and meeting place for Jews during the Nazi

Pharmacy Under the Eagle, now a museum documenting the ghetto years.

occupation. Photographs, film, and documentation record the Ghetto years in these three rooms—the sense of recent, tragic history is palpable. Note the wooden cabinet from the original apothecary still set behind the ticket desk by the main door as you go in. A portrait of Pankiewicz is displayed in the back room, surrounded by letters of thanks written by Holocaust survivors from around the world. 🕐 *30 min. See p 41,* **10**.

7 Schindler's Factory. Now converted (at last!) into one of the city's most popular attractions, this museum set in the former Schindler factory of Spielberg legend is well worth the pricey admission. The main entrance, bearing the sign *Fabryka Oskara Schindlera—Emaila,* looks as you would have seen in the film of the same name. Once you walk through it, you're taken on a journey of how Krakow descended into hell in the 1940s. It's more of a general history, well-conceived with a mock-up of a Polish barbers (with gossip played over the speakers), a recreation to show how a bunker would have looked for the families who had to spend months down there, railway timetables, and models showing the complete abnormality of daily life at the time. 🕐 *1½ hr. See p 42,* **11**.

8 Amon Göth's villa. Close to the Dworcowa tram stop and a drive-in McDonald's lie the wartime sites of Płaszów, the large Nazi forced-labor camp. Up the quiet pathway of Heltmana, this stand-alone house, shabby but not abandoned, was the residence of Amon Göth, the sadistic commander of Płaszów. There is no sign or plaque, just an eerie atmosphere emanating from behind the net curtains. From here, Göth directed operations, shooting and beating random victims on a daily basis. Göth was hanged near here in 1946. 🕐 *10 min. W. Heltmana 22. All trams to Dworcowa.*

9 ★ Płaszów. Spread over a large area behind Amon Göth's villa is the Liban Quarry, where thousands were worked to their deaths. Signs advise visitors to step with reverence across the hilly, overgrown patch of land to the fenced-in site, rundown machinery still visible. If you follow the path from Heltmana 40c, along from Göth's villa, you come to a cross on a plinth and, beyond it, two more plaques. Towering over them rises the massive, stark monument to Płaszów's victims, erected in 1964. Six arms and five lowered heads seem fixed in reverence, visible from the main road between Krakow and Wieliczka. 🕐 *20 min. All trams to Dworcowa.*

Nowa Huta

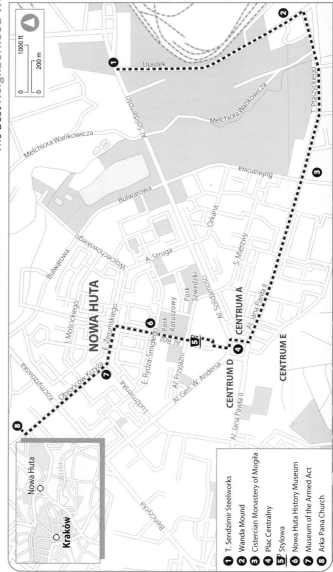

1000 ft
200 m

Ujastek

Melchiora Wańkowicza

Melchiora Wańkowicza

Bulwarowa

A. Struga

Wojciechowskiego

Bulwarowa

Ł.Mościckiego

NOWA HUTA

S. Mierzwy

Orkana

Bulwarowa

T. Ptaszyckiego

Al. Solidarności

S. Żeromskiego

Al. Boż

Park
Ratuszowy

Park
Szwedzki

Al. Solidarność

Al. Jana Pawła II

CENTRUM A

CENTRUM E

E. Rydza-Śmigłego

Lubelniska

Al. Przyjaźni

Al. Gen. W. Andersa

CENTRUM D

Al. Jana Pawła II

Obrońców Krzyża

Kocmyrzowska

Stylowa

Nowa Huta

Kraków

Wisła

Bieńczycka

Bieńczycka

1 T. Sendzimir Steelworks
2 Wanda Mound
3 Cistercian Monastery of Mogiła
4 Plac Centralny
5 Stylowa
6 Nowa Huta History Museum
7 Museum of the Armed Act
8 Arka Pana Church

There is nowhere quite like Nowa Huta, a living, full-scale museum. This brave new world was laid out by Communist planners, wide, straight avenues radiating from an open central square. One leads to the vast steelworks complex around which Nowa Huta was built. Many shops, bars, and restaurants look as they did decades ago. By contrast, the leafy pre-war village of Mogiła a short walk away is an easy, bucolic getaway. START: **Tram 4 to Kombinat.**

❶ ★ T. Sendzimir Steelworks. Renamed after the pioneering Polish metal engineer, the former Lenin Steelworks are vast. Tours (by special arrangement, prices vary) to the 1,000-hectare (2,470-acre) complex are organized on the internal bus system, negotiating roads running for scores of kilometers. Passes can be arranged in advance at the main office by the factory gates—unusually, the management is happy for people to visit, even though the plant is still a working one, employing some 10,000 locals. For most, a photo at the main gates is enough, the factory name spelled out in suitably huge, striking letters. ⏲ 10 min. Tram 4: Kombinat.

❷ ★★ kids Wanda Mound. A 10-minute walk or one stop on the 21 tram takes you from recent history to Krakow's ancient roots. Tucked away through the bushes by the factory fence, this prehistoric manmade hillock is said to be the burial place of Princess Wanda, daughter of the city's mythical founder, the dragon-slayer Krak. An easy climb brings you to the top, marked by a white eagle on a plinth, with a view of the factory complex below. ⏲ 15 min. Tram 21: Kopiec Wandy.

❸ ★ Cistercian Monastery of Mogiła. Another 15-minute walk or a couple of tram stops and you're in the historic village of Mogiła, site of this monastery and church founded in the 13th century. Entering the grand gates, you cross the peaceful, well-kept gardens, to a statue of

The former Lenin Steelworks, now named after T. Sendzimir the Polish engineer.

Nowa Huta by Trabant

You walk into the tiny, dark lobby of the Hotel Floryan at the far end of Florianka in the Old Town. The receptionist rings a number and hands you the receiver. "This is Crazy Mike," says the voice. "When do you want us to come?" Booking a tour with Crazy Guides, organizers of personalized trips to Nowa Huta in original Trabant cars, is not unlike the event itself—random, unpredictable, and bags of fun. At the appointed time, the crazy guide himself—Victor, Bartek, or Mike—arrives at your hotel and gestures to the transport of Commie delight, customized in striking black and red, and embellished with a five-pointed star. You squeeze into the vehicle, one of millions produced in East Germany until 1991, and as you rattle toward Nowa Huta, your guide begins his own history of the area— the riots, the crackdown, the characters. His stories continue as you're taken around Nowa Huta, meeting locals as you do so. The brainchild of Michał "Mike" Ostrowski, a hotel receptionist who started taking guests around in his Polski Fiat, Crazy Guides has expanded from the basic 2-hour tour (119 zł) of Nowa Huta's main sights to include lunch at an original milk bar, visits to his mother's authentically retro apartment, evenings at a 1980s' disco, and even airport pick-ups by Trabbie. A huge success since launching in 2004, **Crazy Guides (www.crazyguides.com)** also runs trips to a traditional farm and visits to Krakow-behind-the-scenes.

St. Bernard of Clairvaux, 12th-century abbot and key figure of the Cistercian order. Take the trouble to walk around the **Abbey Church,** open to visitors—Renaissance murals and an intricate altar of the Madonna and Child are housed in the basilica, embellished with blue stained-glass windows. Across the road, the wooden 15th-century **Church of St. Bartholomew** only opens for mass but visitors may walk around its tranquil grounds.
⏱ *15 min. Klasztorna. Trams 15, 20: Klasztorna.*

4 ★ **Plac Centralny.** All roads (and tramlines) lead to Nowa Huta's main square— grand, spacious, and hexagonal. Controversially named after Ronald Reagan (although still referred to on maps—and by locals—as Plac Centralny), the square is a classic example of Communist planning. The most eminent architects of the day were brought in to landscape an urban design of Renaissance facades and Socialist-Realist housing—four housing estates stand behind the Italianate archways. Arriving from cramped, tourist-swamped Krakow, Plac Centralny feels open and airy, elongated views stretching along its five radial avenues as far as the horizon.

5 ★ **Stylowa.** Opened in 1956, "Style" retains its once-classy-now-retro interior, along with a pleasant beer terrace. Come here and you've definitely been to Nowa Huta. Seen-it-all waitresses in traditional garb serve cheap Polish drinks and standard dishes, with a heavy slice of irony. Breakfasts include herring and smoked salmon; lunchtime tripe, chops, or steaks can be accompanied by the wonderfully named cucumber in cream: *mizeria ze śmietaną. Os.Centrum 3.* ☎ *012/415-80-96. zł.*

⑥ ★ Nowa Huta History Museum. Up focal Aleja Róż from Plac Centralny, this local information office and museum all in one is a useful stop on any tour of Nowa Huta. Staff seem delighted by the arrival of any foreign visitor, breaking out copies of the English-language *Nowa Huta District Guide* and map, and talking visitors through whichever temporary exhibition happens to be staged in the modest space alongside. All have a local theme, so expect posters and black-and-white photographs of heroic workers with backdrops of a Socialist paradise. 🕐 *30 min. Os.Sloneczne 16.* ☎ *012/425-97-75. www.mhk.pl. Admission 5 zł adults, 4 zł children. Free admission Wed. May–Oct Tues–Sun 9:30am–5pm; Nov–Apr Tues, Thurs–Sat, 2nd Sun*

All the roads in Krakow lead to Plac Centralny.

of the month 9am–4pm, Wed 10am–5pm.

⑦ Museum of the Armed Act. Around the corner from the Nowa Huta History Museum stands one of Stalin's IS-2 tanks, one that saw action in World War II. Behind it, renovated and reopened in September 2008, is an exhibition detailing heroic action taken by locals during the conflict. Documents, uniforms, weapons, and medals are displayed

Stalin's IS-2 tank outside the Museum of the Armed Act.

Arka Pana Church.

across one floor, with one section set aside for the wartime letters of Jan Anioła, first director of the steelworks. 🕐 *15 min. Os.Górali 23.* 📞 *691-68-82-27. Free admission. Mon–Fri 10am–3pm.*

8 ★★ **Arka Pana Church.** A fitting end to any tour of Nowa Huta is this quite remarkable church, as astonishing in its construction as it is in appearance. Over the course of 10 years, with no financial or logistical help from the authorities, locals built their church by hand, bringing in 2 million stones bag by bag from the countryside. Work was even stalled by the discovery of 5,000 wartime bombs and shells. Wojciech Pietrzyk's ark-shaped design stands out now as it did upon the church's consecration in 1977, as does Bronisław Chromy's bronze statue of Christ, positioned as if about to fly over the congregation. Set in the tabernacle is a small piece of mineral brought back from the moon by Apollo 11. 🕐 *30 min. Obrońców Krzyża 1.* 📞 *012/644-54-34. www. arkapana.pl. Lower level daily 6–8:30am, 4:30–6:30pm; upper level daily 9am–5pm. No visits during mass. Trams 1, 5: Teatr Ludowy.* ●

Shopping Best Bets

Best Wacky Antiques
★★★ Galeria Osobliwości, *Ul.Sławkowska 16 (p 73)*

Best Hip Designer Clothing
★★★ Punkt, *Ul.Sławkowska 12 (p 72)*

Best Krakow Souvenirs
★★ Galeria Dom Polski, *Pl.Mariacki 3 (p 78)*

Best Gourmet Foods
★★★ Likus Concept Store, *Rynek Główny 13 (p 81)*

Best Vodka Selection
★★★ Szambelan, *Ul.Gołębie 2 (p 81)*

Best Dip into Old-World Krakow
★★ Księgarnia Hetmańska, *Rynek Główny 17 (p 74)*

Best Mall for Kids
★★★ Galeria Kazimierz, *Ul.Podgórska 34 (p 79)*

Best Second-Hand Books in English
★★★ Massolit Books & Café, *Ul.Felicjanek 4 (p 74)*

Best One-Stop Shopping
★★★ Bonarka City Center, *Ul.Kamieńskiego 11 (p 79)*

Best Urban Gear
★ UFO/Underground, *Ul.Floriańska 13;* ★★ Tatuum, *Rynek Główny 37 (p 77)*

Best for International Books & Magazines
★★ Empik, *Rynek Główny 5 (p 73)*

Best Polish Chocolates
★★ Wawel, *Rynek Główny 33 (p 82);* ★★★ Wedel, *Rynek Główny 46 (p 82)*

Best Polish chocolates: Wawel.

Best Amber Jewelry
★★★ Boruni World of Amber, *Sukiennice, Rynek Główny 1/3 (p 78);* ★★★ Ora Gallery, *Ul.Św. Anny 3/1a (p 78)*

Best Postcards & Posters
★★ Galeria Plakatu, *Ul.Stolarska 8–10 (p 78);* ★★ Galeria Autorska Andrzeja Mleczki, *Ul.Św.Jana 14 (p 77)*

Best Contemporary Menswear
★★ Vistula, *Rynek Główny 13 (p 77)*

Best Contemporary Ladieswear
★★★ Hexeline, *Rynek Główny 11 (p 75)*

Best Shoes with Style
★★ Nunc, *Ul.Rakowicka 11 (p 76)*

Previous page: Calik Galeria.

Central Shopping

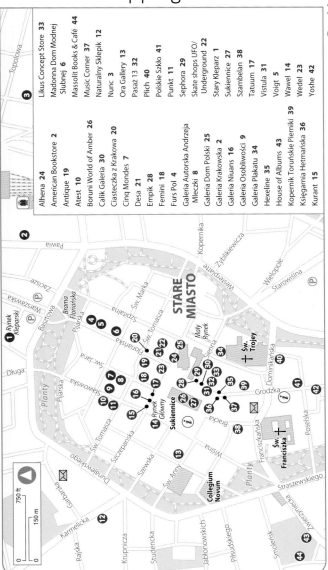

Alhena **24**
American Bookstore **2**
Antique **19**
Atest **10**
Boruni World of Amber **26**
Calik Galeria **30**
Ciasteczka z Krakowa **20**
Cinq Mondes **7**
Desa **21**
Empik **28**
Femini **18**
Furs Pol **4**
Galeria Autorska Andrzeja Mleczki **8**
Galeria Dom Polski **25**
Galeria Krakowska **2**
Galeria Niuans **16**
Galeria Osobliwości **9**
Galeria Plakatu **34**
Hexeline **35**
House of Albums **43**
Kopernik Toruńskie Pierniki **39**
Księgarnia Hetmańska **36**
Kurant **15**

Likus Concept Store **33**
Madonna Dom Modnej Slubnej **6**
Massolit Books & Café **44**
Music Corner **37**
Naturalny Sklepik **12**
Nunc **3**
Ora Gallery **13**
Pasaż 13 **32**
Plich **40**
Polskie Szkło **41**
Punkt **11**
Sephora **29**
Skate shops UFO/ Underground **22**
Stary Kleparz **1**
Sukiennice **27**
Szambelan **38**
Tatuum **17**
Vistula **31**
Voigt **5**
Wawel **14**
Wedel **23**
Yoshe **42**

Kazimierz Shopping

Bonarka City Center **4**
Galeria Kazimierz **5**
High Fidelity **1**
Jarden Jewish Bookshop **3**
Plac Nowy **2**

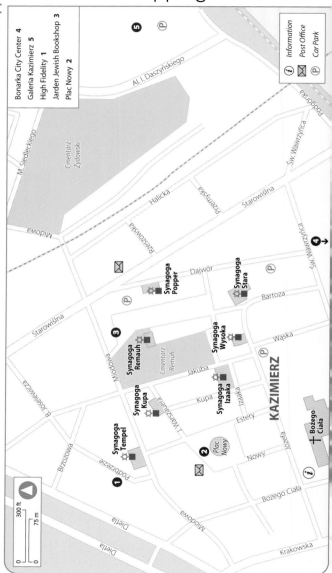

Information
Post Office
Car Park

Krakow **Shopping A to Z**

Antiques & Art

★ **Antique** OLD TOWN Exquisite pieces of art, silverware, porcelain, jewelry, and furniture are arranged around this historic town house. The store is particularly strong on 19th- and 20th-century paintings, and Empire-style furniture. *Ul.Św.Tomasza 19.* ☎ *012/421-79-44. AE, MC, V. All trams to Old Town. Map p 71.*

★ **Atest** OLD TOWN A reliable antiques store where historic items of furniture, jewelry, and cutlery are bought, sold, and assessed by experienced staff who have been working here from time immemorial and are well versed in dealing with foreign customers. *Ul.Sławkowska 14.* ☎ *012/421-95-19. AE, MC, V. All trams to Old Town. Map p 71.*

★★ **Desa** OLD TOWN This chain of atmospheric antiques salons and auction houses holds regular sales. At this chief branch near the main square, you feel welcome to browse the paintings, jewelry, ornaments, cabinets, and sundry artifacts spread over two floors. *Ul.Floriańska 13.* ☎ *012/422-27-06. www.desa. art.pl. AE, MC, V. All trams to Old Town. Map p 71.*

Find curiosities at Galeria Osobliwości.

★★★ **Galeria Osobliwości** OLD TOWN Otherwise known as the Este, this marvelous "Gallery of Curiosities" stocks not only art, furniture, and jewelry but minerals, fossils, African figurines, masks, even a number of didgeridoos. *Ul.Sławkowska 16.* ☎ *012/429-19-84. AE, MC, V. All trams to Old Town. Map p 71.*

Books, Press & Stationery

★ **American Bookstore** NEAR OLD TOWN A relatively recent feature of the Galeria Krakowska mall by the train station, this modest store tries to pack in as many best-sellers as it can within its small space. Refer to the website for other branches in town. *Galeria Krakowska, Ul.Pawia 5.* ☎ *012/628-75-73. www.americanbookstore.pl. AE, DC, MC, V. All trams to Dworzec Główny. Map p 71.*

★★ **Empik** OLD TOWN The former International Book and Press Club today sells travel guides, children's books, maps, novels, and manuals in English and Polish, plus CDs, DVDs, and coffee-table photo albums for special occasions. There's a photo department too, and an Internet cafe upstairs. *Rynek Główny 5.* ☎ *012/429-41-62. www. empik.com. AE, DC, MC, V. All trams to Old Town. Map p 71.*

★ **House of Albums** NEAR OLD TOWN If you're looking for a book as a present, rather than a paperback for the train, then this store is where to find lovely (and expensive) hardback albums. Most of the stock is in Polish but there are many photographic collections. *Ul.Zwierzyniecka 17.* ☎ *012/429-13-63. AE, MC, V. All trams to Jubilat. Map p 71.*

★ Jarden Jewish Bookshop

KAZIMIERZ Hundreds of titles relating to Jewish life, history, and culture are stocked here, many of them in English. Browse recipe books, guides, local histories, novels, and biographies alongside a significant number of volumes on Auschwitz. *Ul.Szeroka 2.* ☎ *012/421-71-66. www.jarden.pl. AE, DC, MC, V. Tram 7, 9, 11, 13, 24: Miodowa. Map p 72.*

★★ Księgarnia Hetmańska OLD

TOWN A fabulous treasure trove, this, in the historic house of the same name. A window display of jigsaw puzzles, globes, pictorial maps, and Krakow-related tomes drags you from the main square into a three-space store of mainly books and attractive souvenirs. *Rynek Główny 17.* ☎ *012/430-24-53. AE, MC, V. All trams to Old Town. Map p 71.*

★★★ Massolit Books & Café

NOWY ŚWIAT This inviting emporium, tucked down a quiet backstreet, is not only Krakow's main purveyor of second-hand books in English but a great cafe, reading room, local resource, and meeting place in one. *Ul.Felicjanek 4.* ☎ *012/ 432-41-50. www.massolit.com. AE,*

Księgarnia Hetmańska.

MC, V. All trams to Jubilat. Map p 71.

China, Crystal & Ceramics

★★★ Alhena OLD TOWN At a

suitably prestigious address, this boutique carries some of the finest examples of local glass, crystal, and silverware. If you're looking for that special cut-glass vase, this is where to come. *Pl.Mariacki 1.* ☎ *012/421- 54-96. www.alhena.pl. AE, MC, V. All trams to Old Town. Map p 71.*

Prime Shopping Zones

You'll find Krakow's finest boutiques for clothes, jewelry, souvenirs, and upmarket goods on focal **Rynek Główny** and the two main streets leading off it north and south, **Floriańska** and **Grodzka.** Nearly 300 retail outlets can be found at the **Galeria Krakowska** (p 79), just off Floriańska by the train station, with half as many now open at the more modest **Galeria Kazimierz** (p 79) in the district of the same name. For fresh produce, the age-old **Stary Kleparz** (p 79) market is a short walk from the station too. The vast and impressive new mall over the river in Podgórze, the **Bonarka City Center** (p 79) encourages shoppers to browse beyond the city center.

★ **Galeria Niuans** OLD TOWN A wealth of beautiful objects for everyday use in the home is on display in this tasteful boutique on the main market square. Items in china, silver, smoked glass, and crystal come by way of Swedish firms Kosta Boda and Orrefors, Haviland from Limoges, and Esteban from Paris. *Ul.Rynek Główny 39.* ☎ *012/429-54-46. www.galerianiuans.pl. AE, DC, MC, V. All trams to Old Town. Map p 71.*

★ **Polskie Szkło** OLD TOWN Ewa Adamczyk's store along the Royal Route stocks an attractive selection of cut-glass artifacts, vases, lights, bowls, and glasses. All purchases are artfully wrapped and make appealing presents. *Ul.Grodzka 36.* ☎ *012/422-57-39. MC, V. All trams to Old Town. Map p 71.*

Cosmetics & Perfumes
★★ **Cinq Mondes** OLD TOWN Jean-Louis Poiroux's exotic treatments and cosmetics include aromatherapies, products for spa and ayurvedic massages, and any number of potions from China, Japan, and India for beautifying the body. *Ul.Św.Jana 20.* ☎ *012/422-39-45. www.beautyboutique.pl. AE, DC, MC, V. All trams to Old Town. Map p 71.*

★ **Sephora** OLD TOWN All the top global brands can be found here, most notably those of Helena Rubinstein, born in Krakow in 1870. You'll also find Sephora's own creams, fragrances, moisturizers, and gift packs. *Florieńska 19.* ☎ *012/421-24-24. www.sephora.pl. AE, DC, MC, V. All trams to Old Town. Map p 71.*

Fashion & Accessories
★★ **Femini** OLD TOWN Local Krakow designer duo Monika Pietrzak-Szlęk and Katarzyna Wilk-Filipowicz

Halina Zawadzka's fashion line at Hexeline.

create some of Poland's most beautifully styled and patterned women's clothing. Striking skirts, blouses, and bridalwear are displayed at this boutique, also stocking items by the Warsaw Young Polish Designers' Foundation. *Ul.Św.Jana 5.* ☎ *012/429-19-83. www.femini.pl. AE, DC, MC, V. All trams to Old Town. Map p 71.*

Furs Pol OLD TOWN Fur coats, wraps, and garments of all types are stocked at this old-school store, here since the year dot on Floriańska. Ladies of a certain age serve clients with experienced aplomb in varnished wood surroundings. *Ul.Floriańska 51.* ☎ *012/422-31-39. AE, DC, MC, V. All trams to Old Town. Map p 71.*

★★★ **Hexeline** OLD TOWN Designer Halina Zawadzka and her team created this brand in the 1980s and now have stores across Europe. Head here for superbly cut clothes in sought-after fabrics, with classic yet modern styling. *Rynek Główny 11.* ☎ *012/429-43-76. www.hexe.com.pl. AE, DC, MC, V. All trams to Old Town. Map p 71.*

★ **Madonna Dom Modnej Slubnej** OLD TOWN Madonna is the city's showcase for Spain's renowned designers Pronovias, and

Award-Winning Design

To see Krakow at its most contemporary and cutting-edge, have a look at the handiwork of radical local clothes designer Monika Drożyńska. This award-winning graduate of Krakow's Jan Matejko Academy of Fine Arts, now in her early 30s, began her trade by creating ad-hoc pieces of clothing out of throwaway items such as curtains and bedspreads. Starting out with a fellow graduate, Monika took her inspiration from the vintage clothing scene she had picked up on in the U.S. They began making clothes for friends, then ran a stall, then opened their boutique in the Old Town, **Punkt** (below). As opposed to the rather staid shop windows on and around the main square, Punkt was funky, fun yet functional—and fabulously original. They still are. Check out Monika's scarves, skirts, and tops.

its San Patrick and La Sposa lines. Veils, necklaces, purses, and other accessories are also on show. *Ul.Floriańska 39.* ☎ *012/422-24-00. www.madonna.pl. AE, DC, MC, V. All trams to Old Town. Map p 71.*

★★ **Nunc** NEAR OLD TOWN Krakow-born Dominika Nowak's creations use natural materials, most notably animal hide—goatskin, cowhide, horse leather. This, her first boutique and concept store, opened in 2006 and presents her seasonal collections. *Ul.Rakowicka 11.* ☎ *012/421-99-55. www.nunc fashion.com. AE, DC, MC, V. All trams to Old Town. Map p 71.*

★★ **Plich** OLD TOWN As exclusive as it gets, Plich is renowned for creating individual pieces to order— original skirts, blouses, and dresses sewn on request, with four-figure euro pricetags attached to them. Considered to be a Polish trademark of style and distinction. *Ul.Dominikańska 3.* ☎ *012/430-19-22. AE, DC, MC, V. All trams to Old Town. Map p 71.*

★★★ **Punkt** OLD TOWN Young designer Monika Drożyńska is responsible for one of Krakow's most exciting and original stores. Expect remodeled vintage clothes and all-purpose handbags that can

Recycled and re-modeled vintage at Punkt.

double up as picnic blankets. See also box, left. *Ul.Sławkowska 12.* ☎ *012/ 502-600-410. http://punkt. sklep.pl. AE, DC, MC, V. All trams to Old Town. Map p 71.*

★ **Skate shops UFO/Underground** OLD TOWN   These two adjoining skate shops, set below the renowned auction house Desa, stock a bright range of urban streetwear—Etnies and DCshoecousa sneakers, baseball caps, wallets, belts, bags, T-shirts—as well as boards and skates. *Ul.Floriańska 13.* ☎ *012/422-54-35. MC, V. All trams to Old Town. Map p 71.*

★★ **Tatuum** OLD TOWN   This domestic brand of casual and contemporary fashion for men and women is one of the country's best exports. Stark white walls bring out Tatuum's bright colors in urban wear at this branch, right on the main market square. *Rynek Główny 37.* ☎ *012/431-27-52. www.tatuum.pl. AE, DC, MC, V. All trams to Old Town. Map p 71.*

★★ **Vistula** OLD TOWN   Krakowbased Vistula is one of Poland's most successful brands of menswear. Original chic, sharp suits, and jackets come with each seasonal collection. A made-to-measure service is also available for gentlemen of size. *Rynek Główny 13.* ☎ *012/ 783-781-341. http://sklep.vistula.pl. AE, DC, MC, V. All trams to Old Town. Map p 71.*

★ **Voigt** OLD TOWN   In business since the turn of the 20th century, and at this prestigious address for 80 years, the original firm of Helen Voigt today stocks the most contemporary glasses and shades in town—Ray-Ban, Police, Marc O'Polo, all the top brands. *Ul.Floriańska 47.* ☎ *012/422-34-62. www.voigt-optyk. pl. AE, DC, MC, V. All trams to Old Town. Map p 71.*

★ **Yoshe** NEAR OLD TOWN   Yoshe produces a select number of ladies' clothes, scarves, purses, and accessories each season. Trendy but accessible, Yoshe's original pieces fill a gap in the market and provide a local alternative amid the global chains in the Galeria Krakowska. *Ul.Pawia 5.* ☎ *012/628-71-59. AE, DC, MC, V. All trams to Dworzec Główny. Map p 71.*

Gifts & Souvenirs

★★ **Calik Galeria** OLD TOWN   If you're visiting in December, call in to this main-square boutique for traditional and original Christmas ornaments. Trinkets in glass, wood, and other materials can be beautifully wrapped and presented. Look out for characters in Polish folk costumes and the irrepressible Krakow dragon. *Rynek Główny 7.* ☎ *012/ 421-77-60. www.calik.pl. AE, MC, V. All trams to Old Town. Map p 71.*

★★ **Galeria Autorska Andrzeja Mleczki** OLD TOWN   If you're looking for something with a personal touch, then the much-loved works of revered cartoonist Andrzej Mleczko should be just the thing. Posters, mugs, and T-shirts feature

Calik Galeria.

the Polish equivalent of The Far Side. *Ul.Św.Jana 14.* ☎ *012/421-71-04. http://mleczko.interia.pl. MC, V. All trams to Old Town. Map p 71.*

★★ Galeria Dom Polski OLD TOWN

The Polish Home Gallery, in the same building as the tourist information office, is a handy stop for tasteful ceramics, candles, animal-shaped objects for everyday use around the home, glassware, and paintings. *Pl.Mariacki 3.* ☎ *012/431-16-77. AE, MC, V. All trams to Old Town. Map p 71.*

★★ Galeria Plakatu OLD TOWN

An interesting store, this, stocking hundreds of local-language film, theater, and circus posters, as well as the work of Poland's most famous exponents of the genre—Sebastian Kubica, Jan Sawka, and Eugeniusz Get-Stankiewicz. *Ul.Stolarska 8–10.* ☎ *012/421-26-40. www.cracowpostergallery.com. AE, MC, V. All trams to Old Town. Map p 71.*

★★★ Sukiennice OLD TOWN

The most prominent—and most picturesque—port of call for your gifts is the Cloth Hall, slap in the middle of the main market square. Stalls of leather goods, folk-inspired artifacts, hats, lace, woodcraft, and sundry souvenirs line the historic hall thronging with tourists. *Rynek Główny. All trams to Old Town. Map p 71.*

Jewelry & Amber

★★★ Boruni World of Amber OLD TOWN

This is one of the biggest local purveyors of amber, offering assorted jewelry and trinkets—including sugar bowls, letter openers, and chess pieces. Items have been intricately crafted with silver and gold to produce artifacts redolent of any visit to Poland. *Sukiennice, Rynek Główny 1/3.* ☎ *012/428-50-86. www.boruni.pl. AE, DC, MC, V. All trams to Old Town. Map p 71.*

★★★ Ora Gallery OLD TOWN

Contemporary designs of amber and rare stones stand out at this jeweler, with necklaces, earrings, pendants, and rings glittering beneath display cases. Not the cheapest boutique of its kind in the city but the quality is reliably good. *Ul.Św.Anny 3/1a.* ☎ *012/426-89-20. www.galeria-ora.com. AE, DC, MC, V. All trams to Old Town. Map p 71.*

Posters galore at Galeria Plakatu.

Look for souvenirs at Sukiennice.

Malls & Department Stores

★★★ Bonarka City Center

PODGÓRZE   The BCC is vast yet tasteful, allowing as much natural daylight as possible to fall upon the 270 retail outlets and 30 restaurants and cafes. Everything is connected by way of little bridges to give the illusion of a city within a city. Outside are spaces for more than 3,000 cars; inside you'll also find a significant cinema complex. *Ul.Kamieńskiego 11.* ☎ *012/298-60-00. www.bonarkacity center.pl. Buses 103, 144, 173, 179, 184. Map p 72.*

★★★ Galeria Kazimierz

KAZIMIERZ   Two floors of more than 100 outlets (Lego, Swarovski, Timberland, Samsonite) are complemented by a modern multiplex cinema and the usual cafe and fast-food outlets. Special buses are laid on for shoppers from Planty and Wawel. *Ul.Podgórska 34.* ☎ *012/433-01-01. www.galeriakazimierz.pl. All trams to Św.Wawrzyńca. Map p 72.*

★★ Galeria Krakowska

NEAR OLD TOWN   Once the main mall in Krakow, this shiny complex by the train station features 270 outlets, with more than a third devoted to fashion—brands include Zara, Versace, Pierre Cardin, and Benetton. There are a dozen sports retailers too, and a selection of fast-food outlets. *Ul.Pawia 5.* ☎ *012/428-99-00. www.galeria-krakowska.pl. All trams to Dworzec Główny. Map p 71.*

★★★ Pasaż 13 OLD TOWN

Krakow's one-stop solution for everything chic, elite, and boutique is this medieval basement lined with the likes of LFC, Vinoteka 13, Likus Concept Store, and the upscale delicatessen Delikatesy 13. *Rynek Główny 13.* ☎ *012/617-02-20. www.pasaz13.pl. AE, DC, MC, V. All trams to Old Town. Map p 71.*

Markets

★★ Plac Nowy KAZIMIERZ

Centerpieced by the former Jewish poultry slaughterhouse of the Rotunda, this open square accommodates some 300 stalls selling fruit and vegetables, flowers, meat, and dairy products. On Sunday mornings, the square is transformed into Krakow's main flea market. *Pl.Nowy. Tram 7, 9, 11, 13, 24: Miodowa. Map p 72.*

★★★ Stary Kleparz NEAR OLD TOWN   It's been here for centuries,

Old school music store Kurant.

this market just the other side of the Old Town ring road. Today around 70 stalls sell fruit and vegetables, flowers, meat, bread, and cheese. Not to be confused with Nowy Kleparz, a more modern marketplace at the far northern end of Ul.Długa. *Ul.Krowoderska 22/5.* ☎ *012/634-15-32. www.stary kleparz.com. Tram 3, 5, 7, 19: Nowy Kleparz. Map p 71.*

Stary Kleparz for local food produce.

Music

★★★ **High Fidelity** KAZIMI-ERZ   Krakow's best trove of second-hand records, CDs, and books is stacked in fruit boxes in this intimate shop in a quiet Kazimierz side street. Great for finding obscure Polish 45s from the 1970s and '80s, handy as kitsch presents for friends back home. *Ul.Podbrzezie 6.* ☎ *0506/18-44-79. All trams to Św.Wawrzyńca. Map p 72.*

★★ **Kurant** OLD TOWN   CDs and books are kept behind glass cases and on behind-the-counter wooden shelves at this old-school music store on the main square. There's a good selection of Polish folk and jazz CDs, as well as music and stories for children. *Rynek Główny 36.* ☎ *012/422-98-59. www.kurant. krakow.pl. MC, V. All trams to Old Town. Map p 71.*

★★ **Music Corner** OLD TOWN The latest pop, rock, jazz, classical, and DVD releases are stocked at this spacious, easy-to-use store on the main square. Also try Empik (p 73) for that recent film or album you're looking for. *Rynek Główny 13.*

Likus Concept Store.

☎ 012/421-82-53. www.music corner.pl. MC, V. All trams to Old Town. Map p 71.

Specialty Food & Drink

★ **Ciasteczka z Krakowa** OLD TOWN   Delicate little cakes, fruit teas, chocolate pralines, and pretty presentation boxes of local sweet treats are all on offer here. *Ul.Św. Tomasza 21.* ☎ *012/423-22-27. www.ciasteczka-z-krakowa.pl. MC, V. All trams to Old Town. Map p 71.*

★★★ **Kopernik Toruńskie Pierniki** OLD TOWN   Nearby Toruń has a tradition of making gingerbread going back centuries. In its main Krakow outlet, you can pick up gingerbread in all kinds of shapes and coatings. Many are nicely packaged in boxes in designs (stars, planets) relating to Toruń's most famous son, Copernicus. *Ul.Grodzka 14–16.* ☎ *012/431-13-06. www. kopernik.com.pl. MC, V. All trams to Old Town. Map p 71.*

★★★ **Likus Concept Store** OLD TOWN   Upmarket delights are stocked in this basement delicatessen in the Pasaż 13 center—chocolates, spirits, candies—mainly sourced from regional manufacturers. *Rynek Główny 13.* ☎ *012/617-02-50. www.likusconceptstore.pl. AE, DC, MC, V. All trams to Old Town. Map p 71.*

★ **Naturalny Sklepik** NEAR OLD TOWN   At the back of a hidden courtyard, this shed-like outlet deals in organic and natural products for the plate and for the body. Staff speak English and are happy to advise you on what you might need. *Ul.Krupnicza 8.* ☎ *012/422-96-83. MC, V. All trams to Teatr Bagatela. Map p 71.*

★★★ **Szambelan** OLD TOWN The best selection of vodkas in town is found here, along with olive oils and sundry preserves. The bottles make ideal gifts—simply pick an attractive shape and have one of the knowledgeable staff here fill it with the concoction of your choice. *Ul.Gołębie 2.* ☎ *012/628-70-93. www.szambelan.com.pl. AE, DC, MC, V. All trams to Old Town. Map p 71.*

The Best Shopping

All That Glitters

Amber has always been one of Poland's key exports. Cities such as Gdańsk and Krakow grew rich during the medieval era on the strength of the amber trade. This "Baltic Gold" is a resin, the fossiled remains from prehistoric forests from the age of the dinosaurs. Occasionally you find amber with small creatures trapped inside it, stuck there for eternity. Treasures created by the Gdańsk guild of amber craftsmen can be found in **Wawel Castle** and **Cathedral** (p 54). It was also traded in the **Sukiennice** on the main square, as a visit to the new **Rynek Underground** (p 25) museum should prove. These days, amber is as fashionable now as it was in the 1700s. To see what the fuss is all about, walk into one of the branches of the renowned jewelry chain **Boruni World of Amber** (p 78) and see how this rare resin is fashioned into beautiful necklaces, earrings, and rings.

★★ **Wawel** OLD TOWN   All kinds of chocolate products are sold at this prominent store—wafers, candies, pralines, cocoa, and boxes for gifts and souvenirs. *Rynek Główny 33.* ☎ *012/423-12-47. www.wawel. com.pl. AE, DC, MC, V. All trams to Old Town. Map p 71.*

★★★ **Wedel** OLD TOWN   One of Poland's best-loved chocolatiers, in business for 150 years, runs this store and elegant cafe on the main square. Wedel is best known for its wonderful pralines—honey, amaretto, rum—sold individually or in presentation boxes. *Rynek Główny 46.* ☎ *012/429-40-85. www.wedel pijalnie.pl. AE, DC, MC, V. All trams to Old Town. Map p 71.* ●

Wedel chocolates decorated with musical notes.

Waterfront

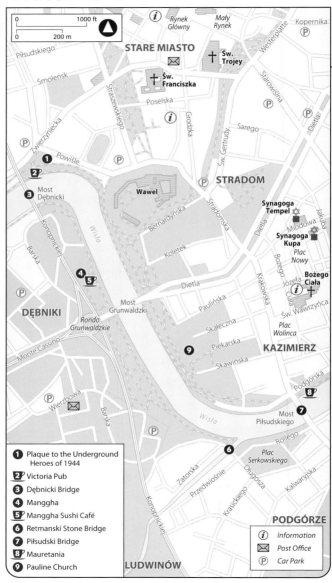

0 — 1000 ft
0 — 200 m

Piłsudskiego

Smoleńsk

STARE MIASTO

Rynek Główny

Mały Rynek

Kopernika

Westerplatte

✝ **Św. Trojey**

Starowiślna

Dietla

✝ **Św. Franciszka**

Poselska

Sarego

Św. Gertrudy

Grodzka

STRADOM

Zwierzyniecka

Powiśle

1

2

3 Most Dębnicki

Straszewskiego

Wawel

Bernardyńska

Stradomska

Synagoga Tempel

Miodowa

Dietla

Synagoga Kupa

Plac Nowy

Jakuba

Bożego

Krakowska

Bożego Ciała ✝

Józefa

Barska

Konopnickiej

Wisła

Koletek

4

5

Most Grunwaldzki

Dietla

Paulińska

Św. Wawrzyńca

Plac Wolnica

DĘBNIKI

Rondo Grunwaldzkie

Skałeczna

Piekarska

9

KAZIMIERZ

Monte Cassino

Skawińska

Podgórska

8

Wierzbowa

Barska

Wisła

Most Piłsudskiego

7

Rollego

Konopnickiej

6

Zatorska

Przedwiośnie

Plac Serkowskiego

Długosza

Krasickiego

Kalwaryjska

PODGÓRZE

LUDWINÓW

1 Plaque to the Underground Heroes of 1944

2 Victoria Pub

3 Dębnicki Bridge

4 Manggha

5 Manggha Sushi Café

6 Retmanski Stone Bridge

7 Piłsudski Bridge

8 Mauretania

9 Pauline Church

(i) Information

✉ Post Office

ⓟ Car Park

Previous page: The Planty.

The **Vistula waterfront is sadly underused.** Couples on the grass slopes beneath Wawel, floating bars, and boat tours are the only immediately obvious activities. But you'll also find contemporary Japanese art, a top-quality sushi bar, and a church linked with a 1,000-year-old legend. And it's all a stroll away from the crowds.

START: **All trams to Jubilat.**

① Plaque to the Underground Heroes of 1944. As you walk toward the Jubilat shopping center from the Sheraton Hotel, cast your eyes away from the river to find this plaque topped by a Polish eagle. It marks the spot where members of the Polish Underground attempted to assassinate SS General Wilhelm Koppe in July 1944, a few days before the attempt on Hitler's life. Having survived, Koppe later ordered the execution of all Polish prisoners before the advancing Soviets. After going underground, Koppe ran a chocolate factory in Bonn and died a free man in 1975. The plaque names the five would-be assassins, giving each of their nicknames. ⏲ *10 min. Powiśle/Zwierzyniecka. All trams to Jubilat.*

Plaque to the Underground Heroes of 1944.

2 Victoria Pub. Just below the Dębnicki Bridge in summer, two boat bars are set up side by side. This is the first one you come to, with two decks of bar space, the outer, upper one giving a pleasant breeze off the river as you sip your draught Okocim. There are modest bar snacks too, and a fridge full of Magnum ice creams. *Powiśle/Dębnicki Bridge. All trams to Jubilat. zł.*

③ Dębnicki Bridge. Compared to Prague or Budapest, Krakow's bridges are prosaic. This one was at least designed to be low enough so as not to obscure the beautiful view of Wawel from the opposite bank. When it was opened in 1952, the bridge connected the southwest of the city with the residential district of Dębnicki. It still does but it also carries traffic from Slovakia and Zakopane away from the Old Town and north toward Kielce and Warsaw—it's busy. Crossing its 157-m (515-ft.) span, your feet are constantly rattling until you reach the eerie calm of the south bank. ⏲ *10 min. Trams 18, 19, 22 to Dębnicki.*

Take a stroll by the Vistula waterfront.

Manggha Sushi Café and terrace.

❹ ★★★ Manggha. The Museum of Japanese Art and Technology is one of Krakow's most underrated treasures, located over the river from Wawel. Many of the items were bequeathed in the 1920s by eccentric art collector Feliks Jasieński to Krakow's National Museum—fabrics, art, wood engravings, and weapons. For little-known reasons, Jasieński dedicated his life to seeking out artifacts from Japan. In storage for decades, the collection caught the interest of film director Andrzej Wajda and his wife, always keen to raise the cultural profile of the city. On their initiative, a riverside center was built here to house Jasieński's artifacts and to host exhibitions by contemporary Japanese artists. Arata Isozaki's light-filled complex is the perfect backdrop for the 7,000-strong permanent collection, shown in rotation, and for diverse temporary shows. Manggha also contains a hall, a terrace cafe, and a sushi bar. ⏱ *1 hr. Ul.Konopnickiej 26.* ☎ *012/267-27-03. www.manggha. krakow.pl. Admission 15 zł adults, 10 zł children. Tues–Sun 10am–6pm. Tram 18, 19, 22.*

5️⃣ Manggha Sushi Café. Some 15 varieties of sushi and a lovely riverside view are on offer at one of Krakow's best museum eateries. Ginger and other types of sake are also available, plus Japanese beers and a range of teas too. *Ul.Konopnickiej 26.* ☎ *012/267-27-03. złzłzł.*

❻ ★ Retmanski Stone Bridge. Wander along the south bank of the Vistula from Manggha, past the Grunwald Bridge and you come to a bend in the river and this little stone bridge. A century old, it is named after the raftsmen who would have used the waterway to trade goods. The scene is bucolic—the quiet Wilga tributary divides Podgórze from the rest of the south bank, where young couples skim stones and old men dangle fishing rods. Slated for redevelopment, the area should be best enjoyed before another leisure complex rises in its place. Another 10 minutes and you arrive at the Piłsudski Bridge and Podgórze proper. ⏱ *10 min. Zator-ska/Przedwiesnie. Trams 8, 10, 11.*

❼ Piłsudski Bridge. Opened in 1933, this cast-iron bridge rises in three arches across the river, allowing views of historic Wawel and newly regenerated Podgórze on either side. ⏱ *10 min. See p 61,* **❶**.

Krakow by Boat

Vistula tours: In summer, a handful of companies run trips along the river, usually setting off from Bulwar Czerwieński on the north bank of the Vistula at the foot of Wawel. The Nimfa makes regular hour-long tours around Krakow (12 zł adults, 10 zł children) or a 3-hour tour to Tyniec (20 zł adults, 15 zł children) at weekends. Check **Żegluga Krakowska** for details (☎ **012/422-08-55,** www.zegluga.krakow.pl). **Sobieski** (☎ **012/452-23-04,** www.ster.net.pl) also runs regular tourist boats to Tyniec and Bielany (2 hr). More haphazard but cheaper river trams (☎ **606/225-555,** www.ktw.krakow.pl) head for Tyniec once there are enough passengers on board.

🚢 Mauretania. Moored by the northern foot of Piłsudski Bridge, this boat bar-restaurant is a handy stop-off from lunchtime to past bedtime. Pastas, salads, seafood, and grilled meats can be accompanied by wine, and followed by an extensive choice of cocktails. Below deck is all wood veneer and maritime-themed decoration—above is a view of Podgórze from the opposite bank. *Bulwar Kurlandzki.* ☎ *692/383-661. www.mauretania.biz. złzł.*

⑨ ★★ Pauline Church. The few who venture down to Kazimierz's far riverside edge are rewarded with this bizarre church and its impressive crypt. On this site in the 11th century, the more modest Church of St. Michael witnessed the brutal murder of Stanisław Szczepański, bishop of Krakow. A curse fell upon the royal family responsible for the deed, giving rise to a multitude of superstitions and a much bigger Gothic church. This in turn was replaced by the imposing baroque church you see today. The crypt contains the tombs of artist Stanisław Wyspiański, composer Karol Szymanowski (1882–1937), and poet Adam Asnyk (1838–97). 🕐 *1 hr. Ul.Skaleczna 15.* ☎ *012/421-72-44. www.skalka.paulini.pl. Daily 9am–7pm. Trams 3, 6, 8, 10, 40.*

The century-old Retmanski stone bridge.

Around the **Planty**

1 Barbican
2 Juliusz Słowacki Theater
3 Café Zakopianka
4 Church of the Dominican Nuns
5 Dominican Church
6 Archaeological Museum
7 Statue of John Paul II
8 Bunkier Sztuki
9 Café Bunkier
10 Palace of Art

(i) Information
✉ Post Office
(P) Car Park

Austrians demolished Krakow's fortified ring in the early 1800s—and Cracovians created a public park in its place: Planty. Bookended by Wawel in the south, these public gardens, a verdant ring of 4km (2½ miles) dotted with monuments, statues, and plaques, encircle the Old Town. Locals sit on park benches, while dog-walkers stroll the paths that criss-cross the grass. START: All trams to Barbican.

❶ ★ **Barbican.** Little accentuates Krakow's medieval appearance, and fear of invasion, more than this once mighty fortress and drawbridge built in the 1400s. The Barbican never saw action and today its grassed-over surrounds allow for a grand entrance into the Old Town from the north, or the ideal starting point for a leafy circumnavigation of Krakow's historic center. ⏱ 20 min. See p 19, ❹.

❷ ★★★ **Juliusz Słowacki Theater.** Krakow's most prestigious concert hall is named after the 19th-century romantic poet and dramatist who died in exile in Paris. A venue for classical music, dance, and theater productions, this ornate *fin-de-siècle* building stands at the northeast corner of the Planty; in the northwest corner, the other side of the Barbican, is a monument to one of Słowacki's heroines, Lilla Weneda. ⏱ 20 min. Pl.Św.Ducha 1. ☎ 012/424-45-00. www.slowacki. krakow.pl. All trams to Lubicz.

❸ **Café Zakopianka.** With its terrace offering a perfect view of the Planty, this historic, arty cafe has been in business since 1834. Snacks, draught Heineken from a huge beer tap, and proper coffee from an elaborate machine from Hamburg-Altona offer sustenance and a continental atmosphere—French decorative touches do the rest. Św.Marka 34. ☎ 012/421-40-45. zł.

Barbican provides a picturesque entrance into the Old Town.

The ornate fin-de-siècle Juliusz Słowacki Theater.

④ ★ Church of the Dominican Nuns. Dedicated to Our Lady of the Snow, this baroque nunnery church was consecrated in 1634, shortly after the convent's conversion from a government building. Its ownership, wrapped up in the politics of 17th-century Krakow, passed from the influential Tarnowski family, who sold it to the wealthy benefactor Anna Lubomirska, keen to find a home for the nuns. Our Lady of the Snow relates to Lubomirska's son, a Polish commander who defeated a stronger Turkish force in battle. Its prime attraction today is an icon of the Virgin dating from around the same time. ⏱ *20 min. Ul.Mikołajska 21.* ☎ *012/431-90-30. Open for services.*

⑤ ★ Dominican Church. This unusual church was built in 1250, shortly after the Dominican order itself was founded. What you see today is a late-19th-century rebuild of the 13th-century Gothic original. Many of the ornate chapels survived an earlier fire, most notably the Myszkowski, with busts of the family

lining the dome. It's very much an active church, with busy services. Some 100 Dominicans live and study here today. ⏱ *30 min.* See p 47, ❼.

⑥ ★★★ Archaeological Museum. Set in grand grounds with Wawel in the background, this former Habsburg prison was opened as a Museum of the Antiquities in 1850. Its collection of Egyptian sarcophagi, figurines, and cat mummies are discoveries made at El Hibeh from the 22nd dynasty. Resins from southern Poland are said to be used in the embalming process, although further explanation is not given. Dark corners reveal displays of coins, masks, and pottery. Another of the three floors of this fusty but fascinating museum contains finds made around the Małopolska region, covering a dizzying array of historic periods. Despite the maps and models, the exhibits are not fully documented and you walk past a blur of swords, bracelets, and pots trying to link the lifelike figures of early man with the tools and jewelry he created. It's all quite intriguing—you walk out to find a sunny spot to sit in the garden, pleased that you'd paid the

The Archaeological Museum's collection of Egyptian artefacts.

modest admission fee but somehow no wiser about Egypt or Małopolska. ⏱ *1 hr. Ul.Senacka 3.* ☎ *012/422-71-00. www.ma.krakow.pl. Admission 7 zł adults, 5 zł children. Free admission Sun. Mon–Wed 9am–2pm, Thurs 2–6pm, Fri, Sun 10am–2pm. All trams to Poczta Główny.*

7 Statue of John Paul II. Several statues have been erected to Poland's greatest modern-day hero around his adopted home town—this one stands in the courtyard of the **Palace of Bishops** where Karol Wojtyła lived as a student, and stayed on his visits as Pope. It was created in bronze soon after his election, by Italian Jole Sensi Croci. Thousands of Cracovians filled the streets around here upon the news of Pope John Paul's death in April 2005. ⏱ *10 min. Ul.Franciszkanska 3. All trams to Filharmonia.*

8 ★★★ Bunkier Sztuki. The Art Bunker is worth a look whatever the time of year—the contemporary agenda of exhibitions at this attractive Modernist building changes regularly and can usually be relied on to be challenging and interesting. ⏱ *30 min. Pl.Szczepański 3a.* ☎ *012/422-40-21. http://bunkier.art.pl. Admission/opening times according to exhibition. All trams to Teatr Bagatela.*

9 Café Bunkier. The finest place to sip coffee or sink a beer on the Planty is this terrace venue attached to the contemporary art gallery of the same name. During cold months, transparent sheets protect customers from the elements, umbrella heaters taking the chill from the bitter Polish winter. In summer, the covers come off and the Bunkier floods with sunlight. Readings and screenings are staged here every now and then. *Pl.Szczepański 3a.* ☎ *012/430-09-71. zł.*

Café Bunkier.

10 Palace of Art. This building, the first example of Art Nouveau in Krakow, harks back to a time in the late 1800s when the city was awash with famous artists—Stanisław Wyspiański, Jan Matejko, and so on. Exhibitions here tend to be more highbrow than the more cutting-edge shows at the Art Bunker nearby—but the building is well worth a look. ⏱ *15 min. See p 30,* **4**.

Palace of Art.

Salwator & **Zwierzyniec**

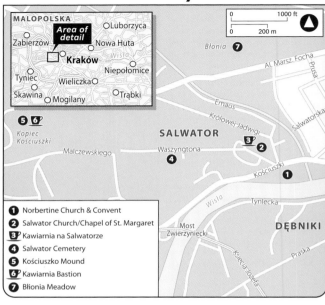

The terminus of three tram routes, Salwator is an easy
jump-off point for a hike into the open greenery of Zwierzyniec,
west of Krakow. Attractions include the Kościuszko Mound and the
cemetery of Salwator, whose steep, crumbling streets were popular
with writers and artists before the war. A bohemian atmosphere still
hangs in the air—that is, until the developers move in. START: **Trams
1, 2, 6: Salwator.**

1 ★ Norbertine Church & Convent. Opposite the tram terminus
by the river stands this partly Romanesque complex, a center for Norbertine sisters since 1148. Its sturdy
appearance harks back to Jagellonian
times when the church needed protection from invaders. White-dressed
canonesses still live here but the
church opens for afternoon services.
This is the starting point for June's
Lajkonik parade. Dating from the Tartar invasions, the carnival is led by a
bearded man in a pointy hat who

leads a crowd in medieval costume
by hobby horse, Monty Python-style.
The procession ends at the market
square. ⏱ *15 min. Ul.T.Kościuszki.
Trams 1, 2, 6: Salwator.*

**2 ★ Salwator Church/Chapel
of St. Margaret.** Climbing steep,
winding Św.Bronisławy, you find two
facing churches: Salwator and the
Chapel of St. Margaret. The former
contains Romanesque elements
and, on the wall of the Presbytery,
frescoes from the 16th century. St.
Margaret's Chapel, a wooden

structure on a hilly slope, dates from the late 1600s. In March 2008, a statue of John Paul II was erected outside. 🕐 *20 min. Św.Bronisławy. Trams 1, 2, 6: Salwator.*

❸ Kawiarnia na Salwatorze. On the steep slope to Salwator Cemetery, this pretty garden cafe offers draught Bitburger, cakes, snacks, and local history. This is the house of Władysław Anczyc (1823–83), the 19th-century Polish poet—the adjoining street is named after him. Imprisoned by the Austrians in 1846, Anczyc was a prominent member of Salwator's artistic community. *Św.Bronisławy/Anczyca 1.* ☎ *501/177-006. zł.*

❹ ★ Salwator Cemetery. As Św.Bronisławy becomes flat, straight, tree-lined Aleja Waszyntona, this quiet cemetery appears on the left-hand side—and with it, a wonderful view of Krakow and beyond. Visit on the **Day of the Dead,** November 1, and the gravestones will be haloed in candlelight. Consecrated in 1865, Salwator contains the tombs of painters and writers who lived here before World War II. 🕐 *30 min. Al.J.Waszyngtona. Trams 1, 2, 6: Salwator, bus 100.*

❺ ★★★ kids Kościuszko Mound. Accessed by the half-hourly minibus 100 from the Salwator terminus, this panoramic attraction contains several features. Foremost is the Kościuszko Mound itself, a conical hill erected in the 1820s in honor of the soldier who fought for Polish and American independence. A spiral staircase leads to the top—it's a dizzying climb. At the foot stands the neo-Gothic **Chapel of Św.Bronisława,** built by the Austrians in the 1850s. Round the corner is a waxworks museum (8 zł adults, 6 zł children), a disappointing collection of Polish heroes in familiar poses. A further

museum beside the Bastion cafe within the mound complex displays the life and achievements of Tadeusz Kościuszko, the development of the mound, and a history of this local phenomenon. 🕐 *1 hr. Al.Waszyngtona 1.* ☎ *012/425-11-16. www.kopieckosciuszki.pl. Admission 10 zł adults, 8 zł children. Free national holidays of Mar 24, May 3 and Nov 11. Daily 9am–dusk. Museum daily 9:30am–4:30pm. Bus 100: Kopiec Kościuszko.*

❻ Kawiarnia Bastion. At the lower slope of the mound is this twin-terrace, open-air cafe, serving drinks and snacks. Overlooking the fortifications, it displays a replica of the Racławice Panorama, the battle scene of the Kościuszko Uprising housed in Wrocław. *Al.Waszyngtona 1.* ☎ *012/425-11-16. zł.*

❼ ★★ kids Błonia Meadow. Signposted from the Kościuszko Mound, this large green space is reached by walking down the winding V.Hofmana to the main Królowej Jadwigi road. Criss-crossed by hiking and cycle paths, the meadow is used by kite-flyers and Frisbee throwers—don't expect cafes or ice-cream stands. 🕐 *30 min. Buses 134, 152, 192, 292.*

Norbertine Church & Convent.

Las **Wolski**

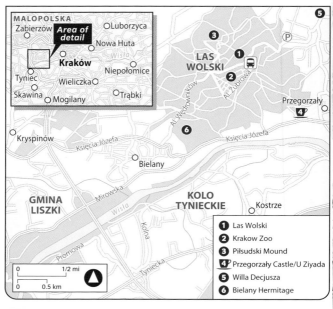

1 Las Wolski
2 Krakow Zoo
3 Piłsudski Mound
4 Przegorzały Castle/U Ziyada
5 Willa Decjusza
6 Bielany Hermitage

The open woodland of Las Wolski contains well-marked hiking trails and a handful of attractions including the city zoo, Przegorzały Castle, and the bizarre Camadulensian Hermitage of Bielany. Regular buses from the city center serve the area—hiking between them would take the best part of a day, no bad way to spend time away from the downtown bustle. START: **Bus 134 to Las Wolski.**

1 ★ kids Las Wolski. Best accessed by the 134 bus, which runs right from the Cracovia Hotel and terminates at its main attraction, the zoo, this 400-hectare (1,000-acre) area of natural woodland was opened for public recreation a century ago. By the entrance to the zoo is a map showing hiking routes, the main sites, and the times it takes to walk to them. From this vantage point you can easily reach the Piłsudski Mound, Przegorzały Castle, and Bielany. ⏲ *2 hr. Bus 134: Zoo.*

2 ★★★ kids Krakow Zoo. Respected internationally as a top breeding zoo, Krakow's animal park has been in business for 80 years. Snow leopards, Andean condors, wild cats, and lynxes have all been raised here in captivity. Local species include boar and bison. A snack bar by the main entrance overlooks the elephant enclosure. ⏲ *2 hr. Las Wolski.* ☎ *012/425-35-51. www.zoo-krakow.pl. Admission 18 zł adults, 10 zł children. Daily summer 9am–7pm; spring, fall 9am–6pm; winter 9am–3pm. Bus 134: Zoo.*

Krakow Zoo wild cat.

3 ★ **kids** **Piłsudski Mound.** A signposted 15-minute walk from the zoo is the tallest and most recent of Krakow's many mounds. Named after the national hero who led the country to independence in World War I, and who died shortly before the mound was finished and opened in 1937, Piłsudski contains soil from the major battlefields where Poles fought between 1914 and 1918. Its size has protected it—both the Nazis and the Soviets wished to raze it. The latter succeeded in removing it from most maps and destroying the tablet laid by the Polish Legion. Prompted by the Solidarity movement, the mound was gradually restored, with soil added from the battlefields of World War II. It was reopened with an elaborate ceremony in 2002. ⏱ *1 hr. Free admission.*

4 **Przegorzały Castle/U Ziyada.** At the far southeastern edge of Las Wolski, located over the river, stands the mock historic Przegorzały Castle. Used for recreation by the Nazis, the castle now contains the restaurant U Ziyada, which serves Polish standards and Kurdish specialties— a hint at the nationality of the current owner. *Ul.Jodłowa 13.* ☎ *012/429-71-05. www.uziyada.krakow.pl. złzł.*

5 ★ **Willa Decjusza.** Although a restaurant—a high-standard and high-priced one at that—Willa Decjusza is worth the detour for non-diners to admire this beautiful 16th-century villa set in lovely grounds on the edge of Las Wolski. ⏱ *15 min.* ☎ *012/425-33-90. www. vd-restauracja.pl. Bus 102, 134, 152, 192.*

6 ★ **Bielany Hermitage.** At the creepy but authentic Bielany Hermitage, women are only allowed on certain feast days—most notably Christmas, Whit Sunday, Easter Sunday, and Easter Monday. Such

Przegorzały Castle terrace.

Bielany Hermitage.

arcane rules echo the Camadulensian order who still occupy the hermitage complex. Men are admitted at 10 specific times between 8am and 4pm, and then only to the hermitage church and crypt. Here the bones of the hermits' predecessors are stacked away in niches, to be buried decades after their passing. The monks lead quiet lives of privation in basic cabins behind the church. ⏱ *30 min.* ☎ *012/429-81-80. Free admission. Bus 109: Bielany.* ●

Practical Matters

If you're in the Las Wolski area, an hour's hike over the Vistula will bring you to **Tyniec Abbey**—there are also day trips straight from Krakow. Tourists come to wander around the 11th-century Benedictine Abbey, spectacularly located over the limestone cliffs at the water's edge. There are also organ recitals here in July and August. Contact the abbey at Benedyktynska 37 (☎ **012/688-54-52;** www.tyniec.benedyktyni.pl).

Dining Best Bets

Best **Breakfast**
★ Jeff's, *Ul.Podgórska 34 (p 104)*

Best **Contemporary Cuisine**
★★★ Ancora, *Ul.Dominikańska 3*
(p 101)

Best **Italian**
★ Aqua e Vino, *Ul.Wiślna 5–10*
(p 101)

Best **Seafood**
★★ Farina, *Ul.Św.Marka 16 (p 103)*

Best **Comfort Food**
★ Bar Grodzki, *Ul.Grodzka 47 (p 102)*

Best **Authentic Jewish Atmosphere**
★ Klezmer Hois, *Ul.Szeroka 6 (p 104)*

Best *Pierogi*
★ Marmolada, *Ul.Grodzka 5 (p 105)*

Best **Reliably Expensive**
★★ Wentzl, *Rynek Główny 19*
(p 109)

Best **Terrace View**
★ Klub Panorama, *Ul.Zwierzyniecka 50 (p 104)*

Best **Pizzeria**
★ Trzy Papryczki, *Ul.Poselska 17*
(p 108)

Best **Polish Regional**
★ Jarema, *Pl.Matejki 5 (p 104)*

Best **Waitstaff**
★★★ Miód Malina, *Ul.Grodzka 40*
(p 105)

Best **Gourmet French**
★★★ Cyrano de Bergerac,
Ul.Słakowska 26, (p 103)

Best **Hotel Restaurant**
★★ Vanilla Sky, *Hotel Art Niebieski & Spa, Ul.Flisacka 3 (p 108)*

Best **Latin American**
★ Manzana, *Ul.Miodowa 11 (p 105)*

Best **Soups**
★ Chłopskie Jadło, *Ul.Św. Jana 3*
(p 102)

Best **Vodka Selection**
★ Baroque, *Ul.Ś. Jana 16 (p 102)*

Best **Salads**
★ Vega, *Ul.Krupnicza 22 (p 109)*

Best for **Extravagant Meat Sauces**
★ Pod Aniołami, *Ul,Grodzka 35*
(p 106)

Below: Vanilla Sky. Previous page: Cyrano de Bergerac.

Central Dining

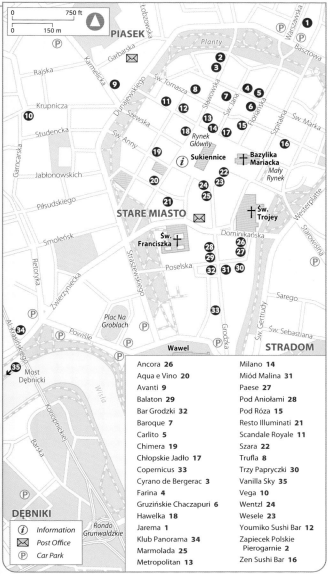

0	750 ft
0	150 m

Ancora **26**
Aqua e Vino **20**
Avanti **9**
Balaton **29**
Bar Grodzki **32**
Baroque **7**
Carlito **5**
Chimera **19**
Chłopskie Jadło **17**
Copernicus **33**
Cyrano de Bergerac **3**
Farina **4**
Gruzińskie Chaczapuri **6**
Hawełka **18**
Jarema **1**
Klub Panorama **34**
Marmolada **25**
Metropolitan **13**

Milano **14**
Miód Malina **31**
Paese **27**
Pod Aniołami **28**
Pod Róza **15**
Resto Illuminati **21**
Scandale Royale **11**
Szara **22**
Trufla **8**
Trzy Papryczki **30**
Vanilla Sky **35**
Vega **10**
Wentzl **24**
Wesele **23**
Youmiko Sushi Bar **12**
Zapiecek Polskie
  Pierogarnie **2**
Zen Sushi Bar **16**

(i) Information
✉ Post Office
Ⓟ Car Park

Kazimierz & Podgórze Dining

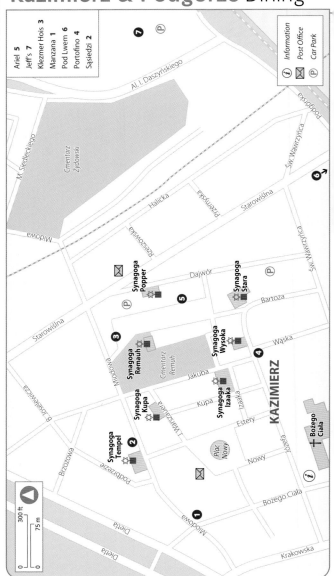

Ariel **5**
Jeff's **7**
Klezmer Hois **3**
Manzana **1**
Pod Lwem **6**
Portofino **4**
Sąsiedzi **2**

Information
Post Office
Car Park

Krakow **Dining A to Z**

Jewish favorites at Ariel.

★★★ Ancora OLD TOWN *CONTEMPORARY POLISH*   Original cuisine is what this destination restaurant delivers, thanks to the deft hand of chief chef Adam Chrzątowski. This former philosophy graduate learned his trade in the top hotels of Warsaw, and had a mission to run his own place in which the cornerstones of Polish cuisine (game, forest fruits, river fish) would be used to create something light, varied, and contemporary. *Ul.Dominikańska 3.* ☎ *012/357-33-55. www.ancora-restaurant.com. Entrees 48 zł–68 zł. AE, DC, MC, V. Lunch & dinner daily. All trams to Old Town. Map p 99.*

★ Aqua e Vino OLD TOWN *ITALIAN*   A suitable candidate for best Italian in town, the creative, contemporary "Water and Wine" specializes in dishes from the Veneto region. This chic eatery also offers quality Italian wines and a selection of cocktails, which can also be enoyed in the lounge bar. *Ul.Wiślna 5–10.* ☎ *012/421-25-67. www.aquaevino. pl. Entrees 22 zł–56 zł. AE, DC, MC, V.*

Lunch & dinner daily. All trams to Old Town. Map p 99.

★ Ariel KAZIMIERZ *JEWISH*   Tourists flock to this homely favorite in the heart of the Kazimierz, partly because of the well-produced Jewish standards (matzoh-ball soup, roast goose, gefilte fish), partly because of the atmosphere akin to a grandmother's drawing room. There are Israeli wines too, kosher vodkas, and Passover *slivovicz* spirit. *Ul.Szeroka 17–18.* ☎ *012/421-79-20. www.ariel-krakow.pl. Entrees 15 zł–65 zł. AE, DC, MC, V. Lunch & dinner daily. Tram 7, 9, 11, 13, 24: Miodowa. Map p 100.*

★★ Avanti BY OLD TOWN *ITALIAN*   Set in the rapidly trendifying neighborhood just outside the Old Town in the student quarter, Avanti comprises a top-quality restaurant, garden cafe, and orangerie with its own extensive menu. The food is sublime, whether grilled prawns on mixed salad, seafood spaghetti with pesto, or the veal in porcini mushroom

Classic, old-school service at Balaton.

sauce. *Ul.Karmelicka 7.* ☎ *012/430-07-70. www.avanti.krakow.pl. Entrees 22 zł–59 zł. AE, DC, MC, V. Late lunch from 3pm & dinner Tues–Sun. All trams to Old Town. Map p 99.*

Balaton OLD TOWN *HUNGARIAN* It's been here for decades, this classic Magyar haunt with its wooden, two-room interior and old-school waiters. The food remains authentic; expect roast duck, wild-boar stew, and bean soup. Prices are as cheap as you'll find for such quality fare so centrally located, and that includes the wines. *Ul.Grodzka 37.* ☎ *012/422-04-69. www.balaton.krakow.pl. Entrees 17 zł–36 zł. AE, DC, MC, V. Lunch & dinner daily. All trams to Old Town. Map p 99.*

★ **Bar Grodzki** OLD TOWN *POLISH* The menu board in English and Polish at this perennial local cheapie tells all. A list of domestic standards, most for under 10 zł, attracts a regular crowd of budget-conscious diners, workers, and backpackers. *Bigos* cabbage-and-sausage stew, pancakes, and *pierogi* all feature, served in a tiled interior decked out with rustic touches. *Ul.Grodzka 47.* ☎ *012/422-68-07. www.grodzki bar.zaprasza.net. Entrees 8 zł–19 zł.*

Carlito's terrace for an ideal summer spot.

No credit cards. Lunch & dinner till 7pm daily. All trams to Old Town. Map p 99.

★ **Baroque** OLD TOWN *INTERNATIONAL* Contemporary cocktail bar and restaurant, where the visitor can opt for a simple pasta dish—black spaghetti with seafood, tagliatelle with salmon and broccoli, or splash out on a hefty and well-presented steak, lamb, or duck. There are classic Polish dishes as well as soups, salads, and pizzas. *Ul.Św.Jana 16.* ☎ *012/422-01-06. www.baroque.com.pl. Entrees 10 zł–58 zł. AE, DC, MC, V. Lunch & dinner daily. All trams to Old Town. Map p 99.*

★ **Carlito** OLD TOWN *ITALIAN* The terrace perched above Floriański is the ideal spot to tuck into pizzas, pastas, or seafood dishes. Big spenders can order duck breast with marsala figs (42 zł), but most are happy to share a four-piece Carlito pizza with friends and enjoy the view. The pretty, expansive interior fills in winter. *Ul.Floriańska 28.* ☎ *012/292-12-12. www.restauracja carlito.pl. Entrees 35 zł–56 zł. AE, DC, MC, V. Lunch & dinner daily. All trams to Old Town. Map p 99.*

kids Chimera OLD TOWN *POLISH* Professors from the nearby university buildings frequent this long-established Polish favorite offering the widest selection of salads in town, although most come for the hearty duck and goose. Children's theater performances are occasionally given on Sunday mornings. *Ul.Św.Anny 3.* ☎ *012/423-21-78. www.chimera.com.pl. Entrees 25 zł–55 zł. AE, DC, MC, V. Lunch & dinner daily. All trams to Old Town. Map p 99.*

★ **Chłopskie Jadło** OLD TOWN *POLISH* With branches all over Poland, and four around Krakow,

Chłopskie Jadło is a reliable purveyor of traditional local cuisine. A vast range of favorites is offered in suitably rustic surroundings—there are 20 soups alone. Specialties include pork roast or ribs, both with Silesian dumplings, and *bigos* stew with mushrooms. If this branch is busy, try the one nearby at Grodzka 9. *Ul.Św.Jana 3.* ☎ *012/429-51-57.* *www.chlopskiejadlo.pl. Entrees 12 zł–49 zł. AE, DC, MC, V. Lunch & dinner daily. All trams to Old Town. Map p 99.*

★★★ Copernicus OLD TOWN *POLISH/COSMOPOLITAN* If director Roman Polański is in town, this is where he dines. Amid frescoes and beneath a Renaissance ceiling, an attentive staff serve superbly conceived seasonal dishes such as veal with marinated tongue on a truffle and potato mousse, or duck with foie gras spiced with marjoram. *Ul.Kanonicza 16, Copernicus Hotel.* ☎ *012/424-34-21. www.copernicus. hotel.com.pl. Entrees 79 zł–89 zł. AE, DC, MC, V. Lunch & dinner daily. All trams to Old Town. Map p 99.*

★★★ Cyrano de Bergerac OLD TOWN *FRENCH* One of the best restaurants in Poland, and certainly the top French table in town, the

Chłopskie Jadło for traditional, local cuisine.

exclusive Cyrano serves banquet-worthy dishes in a historic medieval cellar. Châteaubriand with three-pepper sauce, cognac flambé, and warm fresh vegetables, and St. Jaques scallops with fettuccine and pesto sauce, are typical dishes. *Ul.Sławkowska 26.* ☎ *012/411-72-88. www.cyranodebergerac.pl. Entrees 19 zł–89 zł. AE, DC, MC, V. Lunch & dinner Mon–Sat. Closed Sun. All trams to Old Town. Map p 99.*

★★ kids Farina OLD TOWN *SEAFOOD* Krakow's premier fish restaurant makes imaginative use of imported delicacies from Brittany

Best Hotel Restaurant: Copernicus.

and Italy. Farina specializes in whole fish such as John Dory, Dover sole, or sea bream, baked with garlic and herbs. Order lobster 5 days in advance. The kids' menu (5 zł–14 zł) offers a good choice too. *Ul.Św. Marka 16.* ☎ *012/422-16-80. www. farina.com.pl. Entrees 19 zł–99 zł. AE, DC, MC, V. Lunch & dinner daily. All trams to Old Town. Map p 99.*

Gruzińskie Chaczapuri OLD TOWN *GEORGIAN* Some two dozen Georgian dishes are available at each of Krakow's five branches of the Chaczapuri chain. Cheese, pork, chicken, and aubergine all feature strongly on a menu where little costs more than 20 zł. Vegetarians are well catered for too, with a handful of tasty tomato-and-pepper-based stews. *Ul.Floriańska 26.* ☎ *509/54-28-00. www.chaczapuri. pl. Entrees 15 zł–35 zł. AE, DC, MC, V. Lunch & dinner daily. All trams to Old Town. Map p 99.*

Hawelka OLD TOWN *POLISH* This is the most famous place in town— you're not just here for the pricey beef tenderloins but for the Habsburg ambience and 130-year-old tradition. Salmon, wild boar, and chicken are heavily featured on an extensive menu, but leave room for desserts such as ice-cream soufflé with dried fruit and nuts in cranberry sauce. *Rynek Główny 34.* ☎ *012/428-15-20. www.hawelka.pl. Breakfast, lunch & dinner daily. All trams to Old Town. Map p 99.*

★ **Jarema** NEAR OLD TOWN *POLISH/LITHUANIAN* Specializing in dishes from eastern Poland and Lithuania, this is a lovely, traditional venue on a quiet square just minutes from the Old Town. Tuck into the free appetizer of rustic bread and lard and choose from a well-conceived menu featuring Lithuanian chilled crayfish soup, and blood sausage with onion and apples. *Pl.Matejki 5.* ☎ *012/429-36-69. www.jarema.pl. Entrees 18 zł–49 zł. AE, DC, MC, V. Lunch & dinner daily. All trams to Basztowa LOT. Map p 99.*

★ **Jeff's** KAZIMIERZ *AMERICAN* If you've been in Krakow a while and you're starting to crave baby back ribs or a serious burger, this is where to head. Smiling waitresses serve up hulking portions of beef fillet, lamb chops, or sizzling fajita platters. Golden pancakes, eggs benedict, and French toast all feature on the hangover-killing breakfast menu. *Galeria Kazimierz, Ul.Podgórska 34.* ☎ *012/433-03-30. www.jeffs.pl. Entrees 18 zł–69 zł. AE, DC, MC, V. Breakfast, lunch & dinner daily. All trams to Św.Wawrzyńca. Map p 100.*

★ **Klezmer Hois** KAZIMIERZ *JEWISH* This landmark venue is a cafe, restaurant, theater, hotel, and music venue in one, its three public rooms dressed like a 19th-century drawing room. As concerns the restaurant, Jewish favorites such as *berdytchov* and matzoh-ball soups, stuffed goose neck, and cholent all feature, complemented by salads from turnip to horseradish. *Ul.Szeroka 6.* ☎ *012/411-12-45. www.klezmer.pl. Entrees 17 zł–47 zł. AE, DC, MC, V. Lunch & dinner daily. Tram 7, 9, 11, 13, 24: Miodowa. Map p 100.*

★ **Klub Panorama** NOWY ŚWIAT *POLISH* Hands-down best terrace view in Krakow, the aptly named Panorama sits atop the riverside Jubilat shopping center. The management could double the prices and still be justified—most meat and fish dishes here are in the 20 zł range. Take in the sunset with one of 30 cocktails. *Ul.Zwierzyniecka 50, Jubliat shopping center.* ☎ *012/422-28-14. www.panoramaklub.eu. Entrees 15 zł–53 zł. AE, DC, MC, V. Lunch & dinner daily. All trams to Jubilat. Map p 99.*

★ **Manzana** KAZIMIERZ *MEXICAN/ INTERNATIONAL* One-half cocktail bar, one-half restaurant, 'Apple' is a chic new Latin American venue. A basic five dishes of fish and meat are complemented by a handful of soups, salads, and appetizers. Watch out for the weekend specials, such as mussels in spicy sauce, and side dishes such as marinated fresh spin-ach. *Ul.Miodowa 11.* ☎ *012/422-22-77. www.manzana.com.pl. Entrees 22 zł–99 zł. AE, DC, MC, V. Breakfast, lunch & dinner daily. Tram 7, 9, 11, 13, 24: Miodowa. Map p 100.*

★ **Marmolada** OLD TOWN *POLISH/ ITALIAN* This pleasant, simple, and affordable establishment provides filling but tasty Italo-Polish dishes. Noodles and dumplings are the spe-cialties here, as well as *pierogi* pan-cakes—you won't leave hungry, that's for sure. There's also live music on weekends, although the atmo-sphere is warm here every night of the week. *Ul.Grodzka 5.* ☎ *012/396-49-46. www.marmoladarestauracja. pl. Entrees 15 zł–52 zł. AE, DC, MC, V. Lunch & dinner daily. All trams to Old Town. Map p 99.*

★ 🧒 **Metropolitan** OLD TOWN *COSMOPOLITAN* South African chef Des Davies runs this downtown,

Miód Malina for great food and service.

Cosmopolitan cuisine at Metropolitan.

cosmopolitan bar-diner, where breakfast is as popular as lunch and dinner. Fry-ups to classic American burgers boast a quality of presenta-tion while Asian touches figure throughout, such as in the spicy Thai noodles. Look out for the house fish soup, a delicious mix of sea-food, saffron, and Pernod. *Ul.Sławkowska 3.* ☎ *012/421-98-03. www.metropolitan-krakow.pl. Entrees 18 zł–64 zł. AE, DC, MC, V. Breakfast, lunch & dinner daily. All trams to Old Town. Map p 99.*

★★ **Milano** OLD TOWN *ITALIAN* A change of restaurants at the five-star Pałac Bonerowski Hotel off the main square. The menu, created by chef Grzegorz Fic, concentrates on Italy, with plenty of seafood, all reas-suringly expensive and exquisitely presented. Fresh fish—sea perch, gil-thead, turbot—is the main feature on Thursdays and Fridays. *Ul.Św.Jana 1, Hotel Pałac Bonerowski.* ☎ *012/374-13-00. Entrees 49 zł–65 zł. AE, DC, MC, V. Lunch & dinner daily. All trams to Old Town. Map p 99.*

★★★ **Miód Malina** OLD TOWN *POLISH* The lines outside the front door year round are no coincidence—reserve a table or miss out on one of Krakow's finest meals. And it's not just the woodstove-prepared roasted pork knuckle or sweet marinated spare ribs—the staff are sweethearts. Finish off your meal with a traditional Polish cheesecake, served warm. *Ul.Grodzka 40.* ☎ *012/430-04-11. www.miod malina.pl. Entrees 26 zł–45 zł. AE, DC, MC, V. Lunch & dinner daily. All trams to Old Town. Map p 99.*

★ **Paese** OLD TOWN *CORSICAN* Poland's only Corsican restaurant has been in business for 2 decades, serving Calvi-style filet mignon with Roquefort sauce and African catfish to four rooms of satisfied diners. The outstanding main dish (for three) is a beef fondue, and there are four vegetarian dishes too. Leave room for *fiadone*, Corsican cheesecake with rum. *Ul.Poselski 24.* ☎ *012/421-62-73. www.paese.com. pl. Entrees 19 zł–39 zł. AE, DC, MC, V. Lunch & dinner daily. All trams to Old Town. Map p 99.*

★ **Pod Aniołami** OLD TOWN *POLISH* This is local fare at its most rich and opulent, prepared in a beech-wood oven. Game is well represented—wild boar with beech-smoked bacon, red cabbage, and grilled pepper, and saddle of doe with cognac, stewed mushrooms, red cabbage, and raisins in wine.

The beautiful setting, within an 18th-century Old Town building with a courtyard garden, adds to the attraction. *Ul.Grodzka 35.* ☎ *012/ 421-39-99. www.podaniolami.pl. Entrees 26 zł–64 zł. AE, DC, MC, V. Lunch & dinner daily. All trams to Old Town. Map p 99.*

Pod Lwem PODGÓRZE *POLISH* Another newbie in the Podgórze hub, the modest Pod Lwem touts itself as a "cafe lunch bar." From a breakfast of omelets or toasted sandwiches, this simple establishment then provides pasta or salad dishes almost universally priced at 16 zł each, with a short selection of more substantial mains such as salmon fillet and chuck steak. Dinner is served too, but this is much more of a daytime operation. *Ul.Józefińska 4.* ☎ *012/519-374-737. Entrees 8 zł–26 zł. AE, DC, MC, V. Breakfast, lunch & dinner daily. All trams to Korona/Limanowskiego. Map p 100.*

Pod Róza OLD TOWN *POLISH/ INTERNATIONAL* This hotel restaurant exudes suitable grandeur, located in a leafy, light-filled atrium dominating the lobby. The menu is seasonal, mainly Polish, with plenty of game and mushrooms in the fall and salads in summer. Don't miss

Tempting dessert at Resto Illuminati.

out on dessert—warm chocolate cake with pineapple mousse, lemon cake with mascarpone cream, or a selection of homemade sorbets. *Ul.Floriańska 14, Hotel Pod Róza.* ☎ *012/424-33-00. www.hotel podroza.com. Entrees 35 zł–115 zł. AE, DC, MC, V. Lunch & dinner daily. All trams to Old Town. Map p 99.*

Portofino KAZIMIERZ *ITALIAN/POL-ISH* With a sun-catching terrace, Portofino cannot fail to capture regular passing trade—but the number of return customers indicates the quality of its cuisine. It's not cheap—there's a special weekend menu at 35 zł, designed for diners to linger—but dishes such as braised veal tongue with morel mushroom sauce, and lamb hock baked in aromatic goat's cheese sauce, will have you recommending the place to others. *Wąska 2.* ☎ *012/421-05-37. www.portofino. pl. Entrees 17 zł–65 zł. AE, DC, MC, V. Lunch & dinner daily. Tram 7, 9, 11, 13, 24: Miodowa. Map p 100.*

★★ Resto Illuminati OLD TOWN *INTERNATIONAL* Fresh ingredients are the cornerstone of this contemporary newbie, run by Irish co-owner and chef Michael Conney. The menu isn't extensive but it's seasonal and well-sourced. All takes place in a pleasant, contemporary atmosphere, occasionally accompanied by a pianist tinkling out tunes to suit a well-heeled clientele. Look out for the daily specials chalked up on the blackboard. *Ul.Gołębie 2.* ☎ *012/430-73-73. www.resto illuminati.pl. Entrees 25 zł–63 zł. AE, DC, MC, V. Lunch & dinner daily. All trams to Old Town. Map p 99.*

Sąsiedzi KAZIMIERZ *POLISH* "Neighbors" is a homely, rustic eatery serving well-presented Polish classics on three levels. The most atmospheric is the bare-brick and

---

Trzy Papryczki for fantastic pizzas and imaginative veggie options.

candlelit cellar, where couples can find a cozy alcove before tucking into a starter of mozzarella in yogurt sauce or mushroom soup, followed by veal in sage, ribs in honey sauce, or poached trout in vegetables. *Miodowa 25.* ☎ *500/033-218. Entrees 11 zł–80 zł. AE, DC, MC, V. Lunch & dinner daily. Tram 7, 9, 11, 13, 24: Miodowa. Map p 100.*

Scandale Royale OLD TOWN *POLISH/INTERNATIONAL* This plush restaurant and cocktail bar covers many bases from breakfast to way past bedtime. A late-night tapas menu includes filet of cod in a chorizo crust and shrimps with garlic, while mains feature breast of guinea fowl with green-pepper and white-wine sauce, and risotto with black truffles. There's a children's menu, too, standard cocktails, and imaginative alcoholic shakes. *Pl.Szczepański 2.* ☎ *012/422-13-33. www.lescandale.pl. Entrees 18 zł–57 zł. AE, DC, MC, V. Breakfast, lunch & dinner Mon–Sat. All trams to Old Town. Map p 99.*

Szara OLD TOWN *POLISH/INTERNA-TIONAL* One of the most famous places in town, with a sister branch in Kazimierz, "Gray" provides a constant turnover of tourists with hefty portions of duck, veal, or beef lavished with wine or fruit sauces. Specialties include the starter of smoked reindeer tartar with horse-radish, porcini mushroom cream soup, and a bouillabaisse available in two sizes. There's also a separate bar if you're just after a drink and a bite on the market square. *Rynek Główny 6.* ☎ *012/421-66-69. www.szara.pl. Entrees 37 zł–71 zł. AE, DC, MC, V. Lunch & dinner daily. All trams to Old Town. Map p 99.*

★ **Trufla** OLD TOWN *CONTEMPO-RARY* Customers in this narrow, fashionably decorated dining room peruse the handwritten menu featuring daily-changing specials such as feta or goat's-cheese salad, two sizes of goulash, or chicken filets. It's not revolutionary cuisine, but it is tasty and well-presented. Trufla also opens early enough for coffee and a snack in the morning. *Ul.Św. Tomasza 2.* ☎ *012/422-16-41. Entrees 16 zł–40 zł. AE, DC, MC, V. Breakfast, lunch & dinner daily. All trams to Old Town. Map p 99.*

★ **Trzy Papryczki** OLD TOWN *PIZ-ZAS* Commonly acknowledged to dish up the best pizzas in town, the "Three Peppers" uses all kinds of ingredients to flavor their famous pies. Most come in two sizes, and are priced between 20 zł and 30 zł. There are soups, salads, pastas, and meat dishes, as well as imaginative vegetarian options—aubergine filled with spinach and tomato, for example. *Ul.Poselski 17.* ☎ *012/292-55-32. www.trzypapryczki.krakow.pl. Entrees 17 zł–29 zł. AE, DC, MC, V. Lunch & dinner daily. All trams to Old Town. Map p 99.*

★★ **Vanilla Sky** SALWATOR *MEDI-TERRANEAN* This most discerning choice is where light, creative, mainly Mediterranean cuisine is served in contemporary surroundings, with a lovely terrace view to boot. Well-sourced, local ingredients are used in soups such as white asparagus with ham, and mains such as organic chicken breast with potato-and-truffle sauce, and duck breast in cherry-and-rosemary sauce with fried apples. *Ul.Flisacka 3.*

Vanilla Sky.

Add-Ons

Gratuities: Nearly all diners like to leave a tip as thanks for good service. Yet in Krakow this relatively straightforward and good-natured gesture is rife with pitfalls. First of all, simply saying "thank you" when you're handing over your money, say a large note for a relatively modest required sum, might tell your waiter or waitress that all of the change due back is theirs. Also, it is not always possible to add on the usual 10% tip when paying by credit card—either the machine won't allow it or the extra goes straight to the management. The easiest way is to leave an approximate 10% of the check, in cash, on the table—perhaps making your waiter or waitress aware that it's there, so that no one else takes it!

☎ 012/297-40-05. www.niebieski. com.pl. Entrees 38 zł–59 zł. AE, DC, MC, V. Lunch & dinner daily. Tram 1, 2, 6: Salwator Pętla. Map p 99.

★ **Vega** NEAR OLD TOWN *VEGETARIAN* Krakow's prime meat-free restaurant takes its mission seriously. Vega displays a large spread of salads, behind which a board shows the half-dozen suggestions for a main dish, Including stuffed peppers, pancakes, or *pierogi*. Nothing will cost more than 10 zł. Salads are sold in two sizes, and can be accompanied by over 30 types of tea—there are little fruit cocktails too. *Ul.Krupnicza 22.* ☎ 012/430-08-46. Entrees 9 zł–16 zł. AE, DC, MC, V. Lunch & dinner daily. All trams to Old Town. Map p 99.

★★ **Wentzl** OLD TOWN *POLISH* Beneath a sign dated 1792, this gourmet fixture on the market square is known for its signature recipes, often game marinated in an extravagant fruit-based sauce. Curiosities among the soups and starters include mosaic of shark in Parma ham with citrus sauce, and cappuccino cream of artichoke. All is served beneath timber beams in heritage surroundings. *Rynek*

Główny 19. ☎ 012/429-57-12. www. wentzl.pl. Entrees 58 zł–68 zł. AE, DC, MC, V. Lunch from 1pm & dinner daily. All trams to Old Town. Map p 99.

★★ **Wesele** OLD TOWN *POLISH* From the people behind the reputable Miód Malina on Grozdka (p 105), this rustic eatery ('The Wedding') deals in classic Polish dishes, including the stand-out goose breast, presented in a range of tasty sauces. Occasionally they lay on a few singers putting traditional local folk songs through their paces, but the atmosphere on the two floors is a jovial one, even on quieter evenings. *Rynek Główny 10.* ☎ 012/422-74-60. www.weselerestauracja.pl. Entrees 16 zł–64 zł. AE, DC, MC, V. Lunch & dinner daily. All trams to Old Town. Map p 99.

Youmiko Sushi Bar OLD TOWN *JAPANESE* In this minimalist-style eatery, delicate shapes of rice, fish, and vegetables are created to order, half the fun being watching the expert chef prepare your *hosomaki*, *futomaki*, or *nigiri*. Varieties run from a basic cucumber *hosomaki* to an *unagi* of grilled eel, omelet, and asparagus. A delivery service is also available. *Ul.Szczepański 7.* 012/ *421-26-99. www.youmiko-sushi.pl. Entrees 20 zł–63 zł. AE, DC, MC, V. Lunch & dinner daily. All trams to Old Town. Map p 99.*

Zapiecek Polskie Pierogarnie

OLD TOWN *POLISH*   Another local Old Town cheapie, this *pierogi* place dishes out steaming bowls of dumplings from a little hatch. Zapiecek is anything but sloppy though—the wooden interior is kept clean, the *pierogi* (sweet or savory) is prepared to traditional recipes. Also, it is a rare round-the-clock business. *Ul.Sławkowska 32.* 012/422-74- *95. www.zapiecek.eu. Entrees 8 zł– 10zł. No credit cards. 24 hr daily. All trams to Old Town. Map p 99.*

Zen Sushi Bar

OLD TOWN *JAPA- NESE*   The newest of Krakow's sushi venues, Zen attempts to be as authentic as possible, with a dining area upstairs where diners kneel on a *tatami* floor. In the intimate downstairs section, dishes are categorized by color according to price, claret and gold being the most expensive. A green plate (20 zł) features treats such as gilthead, eel, and sea bass *nigiri,* and *maki* of salmon, avocado, and Japanese mayonnaise. *Ul.Św.Tomasza 29.* 012/426-55-55. www.zensushi.pl. *Entrees 20 zł–200 zł. AE, DC, MC, V. Lunch & dinner daily. Map p 99.* ●

Nightlife Best Bets

Best Bar for Music
★★ Frantic, *Ul.Szewska 5 (p 119)*

Best Microbrewery
★ C.K. Browar, *Ul.Podwale 6–7 (p 115)*

Best Gay Entertainment
★★★ Klub Cocon, *Ul.Gazowa 21 (p 120)*

Best Parisian-Styled Bar
★★★ Les Couleurs, *Ul.Estery 10 (p 116)*

Best Summer Terraces
★★ Mleczarnia, *Ul.Meiselsa 20 (p 116)*; ★ Cudowne Lata, *Ul.Karmelicka 43 (p 115)*

Best Classic Cocktails
★★ Moment, *Ul.Józefa 26 (p 117)*

Best Retro Style
★★★ Łubu Dubu, *Ul.Wielopole 15 (p 120)*; ★ Cztery Pokoje, *Ul.Gołębie 6 (p 115)*

Best Theme Bar
★★★ Propaganda, *Ul.Miodowa 20 (p 117)*

Best River View
★★★ Drukarnia, *Ul.Nadwiślańska 1 (p 115)*

Best Female-Friendly Bar
★★ Miejsce, *Ul.Estery 1 (p 116)*

Best Irish Pub
★ Nic Nowego, *Ul.Św.Krzyża 15 (p 117)*

Best Atmosphere
★★★ Piękny Pies, *Ul.Sławkowska 6a (p 120)*; ★★★ Singer, *Ul.Estery 20 (p 118)*

Best Gay/Straight Mix
★★★ Kitsch, *Ul.Wielopole 15 (p 120)*

Best Quality DJs
★ Cień, *Ul.Św.Jana 15 (p 118)*; ★★ Frantic, *Ul.Szewska 5 (p 119)*

Best Bar Chatter
★★ Dym, *Ul.Św.Tomasza 13 (p 115)*; ★ Migrena, *Ul.Gołębie 3 (p 116)*

Below: Best Female-Friendly Bar: Miejsce. Previous page: Propaganda bar.

Central Nightlife

Awaria **19**
Błędne Kolo **12**
Boom Bar Rush **11**
Cień **15**
C.K. Browar **3**
Cudowne Lata **2**
Cztery Pokoje **10**
Dym **14**
Enso **1**
Frantic **6**
Kijów Club **4**
Kitsch **21**
Klub Ministerstwo **16**
Lubu Dubu **20**
Migrena **9**
Młoda Nowa Polska **13**
Music Bar 9/Light Box Gallery **5**
Nic Nowego **17**
Paparazzi **18**
Piękny Pies **7**
Rdza **8**

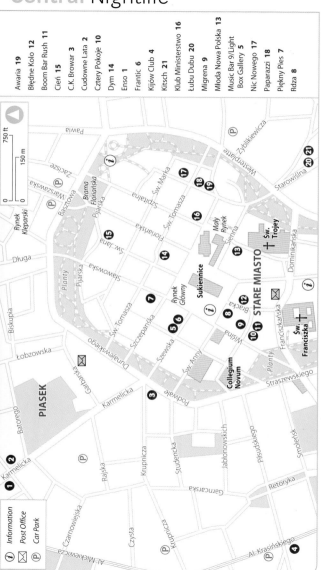

Information
Post Office
Car Park

Kazimierz & Podgórze Nightlife

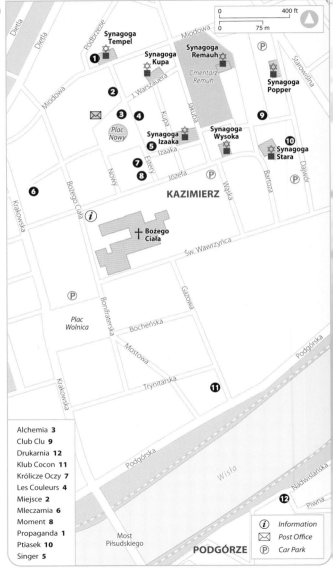

Alchemia **3**
Club Clu **9**
Drukarnia **12**
Klub Cocon **11**
Królicze Oczy **7**
Les Couleurs **4**
Miejsce **2**
Mleczarnia **6**
Moment **8**
Propaganda **1**
Ptasiek **10**
Singer **5**

Krakow Nightlife A to Z

Bars & Pubs

★★ Alchemia KAZIMIERZ   The bar that started the Kazimierz craze, Alchemia can still shake a thing or two—it'll be packed to the gills most weekends until 4am. A long, scuffed wooden interior is entered via the bar area, where drinks must be ordered and picked up. In summer, grab an outdoor table at this busy corner of Plac Nowy before the crowds get here. *Ul.Estery 5.* ☎ *012/421-22-00. www.alchemia. com.pl. Tram 7, 9, 11, 13, 24: Miodowa. Map p 114.*

★ C.K. Browar NEAR OLD TOWN Krakow's main microbrewery bar is a commendably rowdy affair, groups of local lads laying into the house ale by the chunky glassful. The brews, concocted in massive copper vats, include dark, wheat, and ginger varieties. There's food too—platters of ribs, chops, and cutlets. DJs spin at weekends and soccer games are shown on big screens. *Ul.Podwale 6–7.* ☎ *012/429-25-05. www.ckbrowar.pl. All trams to Teatr Bagatela. Map p 113.*

★ Cudowne Lata NEAR OLD TOWN   The slowly burgeoning University Quarter is becoming the place to be—as proven by the popularity of this student-friendly bar. The "Wonder Years" appeals to the kind of person happy with a dark Żywiec in front of them, and not fussed if there are holes in the table doilies. A lively musical backdrop is piped out to the fenced-in front garden in summer. *Ul.Karmelicka 43.* ☎ *012/632-27-29. All trams to Batorego. Map p 113.*

★ Cztery Pokoje OLD TOWN "Four Rooms" is one of the best options for late-night fun in the Old Town. Decorated with retro swirls, it's filled with pretty young things sucking beer through a straw or hitting the bright Kamikaze shots. Well-chosen music plays throughout and this is as good a place as anywhere to try out the local barman's cocktail-mixing skills—a Mojito will set you back 11 zł. *Ul.Gołębie 6.* ☎ *012/ 421-10-14. All trams to Old Town. Map p 113.*

★★★ Drukarnia PODGÓRZE   The move of the legendary Drukarnia bar from Kazimierz to Podgórze in 2007 signaled a major shift in Krakow's geographical hierarchy—before that no one would have had any reason to cross the river. Now this laid-back waterfront cafe fills up every day from lunchtime, regulars spilling onto the pavement outside. It's also a jazz venue, with occasional concerts, but most come here for beer, gossip, and the bohemian atmosphere. *Ul.Nadwiślańska 1.* ☎ *012/656-65- 60. www.drukarnia_podgorze. republika.pl. All trams to Korona/ Limanowskiego. Map p 114.*

★★ Dym OLD TOWN   Of the cluster of venues touching terraces in this quiet little courtyard corner of the Old Town, Dym attracts the most barflies. They gather along the narrow bar counter or at a table in the equally modest front room, filling the air with chatter and *dym* (smoke) until midnight. After that everyone, including the bar staff, staggers off to Piękny Pies. *Ul.Św. Tomasza 13.* ☎ *012/429-66-61. All trams to Old Town. Map p 113.*

★ Królicze Oczy KAZIMIERZ   This thoroughly recommendable spot on Plac Nowy is not the intimate, bohemian, hedonist hang-out of lore, but is still well worth a look-in nonetheless. Now making use of a back-room space and attracting a more

French-style cafe Les Couleurs.

mainstream type of visitor, the "Rabbit's Eyes" features a lively buzz most nights of the week amid mildly erotic decor. It's also a good place to pick up leaflets and flyers for happenings around Kazimierz. *Ul.Estery 14.* ☎ *012/431-10-31. Tram 7, 9, 11, 13, 24: Miodowa. Map p 114.*

★★★ Les Couleurs KAZIMIERZ Probably the best bar on Plac Nowy, "Colors" is a French-style cafe with an imposing zinc bar counter, banquettes, and pleasing touches of Francophilia—old theater posters, Serge Gainsbourg paraphernalia, and a big bottle of Pernod behind the bar. By day, regulars enjoy

Retro venue Miejsce.

breakfast and check their e-mails. By the evening, beers flow and the chat gets loud. *Ul.Estery 10.* ☎ *012/429-42-70. Tram 7, 9, 11, 13, 24: Miodowa. Map p 114.*

★★ Miejsce KAZIMIERZ Probably the most female-friendly of the Plac Nowy bars, this bare, retro venue rarely attracts idiots on stag nights—the gray door is too obscurely signposted. Inside, a vintage TV, Commie-era film posters, and a few strange lamps surround an intelligent, young crowd, intent on discussing culture and the issues of the day rather than diving into wanton hedonism. *Ul.Estery 1.* ☎ *0783/09-60-16. www.miejsce.com.pl. Tram 7, 9, 11, 13, 24: Miodowa. Map p 114.*

★ Migrena OLD TOWN Two bars stand side by side here: one named after the house address itself, and this one named after a particularly bad headache. Both are small, arty, and bohemian in style, and filled with sturdy wooden furniture—Migrena stands out because of the impressive model of Krakow crowning its bar counter. Both make a handy pit-stop on any Old Town bar crawl—especially if you're bound for Cztery Pokoje (p 115) across the street. *Ul.Gołębie 3.* ☎ *012/430-24-18. All trams to Old Town. Map p 113.*

★★ Mleczarnia KAZIMIERZ Krakow's only real beer terrace is set at one end of the famous courtyard Spielberg shot in *Schindler's List*—a relaxing and historic location. Across Meiselsa is Mleczarnia's other spot, a tiny bar filled with bric-a-brac, its doorway open onto the street. This is Krakow at its most bohemian, obscure, random, and irresistible. *Ul.Meiselsa 20.* ☎ *012/421-85-32. www.mle.pl. Tram 7, 9, 11, 13, 24: Miodowa. Map p 114.*

★ Młoda Nowa Polska OLD TOWN This underrated music bar stands close to the Maly Rynek, three rooms with walls covered in newspaper articles. It looks like it would be more at home in Kazimierz, except for the big TV for soccer, the darts machine, and the tap of Murphy's, attracting a handful of expats to join the young, local crowd. A good choice of music is another key factor. *Ul.Stolarska 1.* ☎ *012/422-29-49. All trams to Old Town. Map p 113.*

★★ **Moment** KAZIMIERZ   The best of the relatively new bars on and around Plac Nowy, with a distinctive "time" theme in the design. A convenient spot for breakfast after 9am, Moment comes into its own after dark when well-sourced music serves as the aural backdrop for discerning drinking. The image outdoors of Audrey Hepburn and Gregory Peck cuddling on a moped in *Roman Holiday* is simply inspired. *Ul.Józefa 26.* ☎ *0668/034-000. www.momentcafe.pl. Tram 7, 9, 11, 13, 24: Miodowa. Map p 114.*

★ **Nic Nowego** OLD TOWN   The best of Krakow's Irish bars is a cut above—the contemporary decor, the retro local photography, and the laudable policy of refusing stag parties. A range of quality spirits stands behind the bar—vodkas, gins, whiskeys—near the tap providing the best Guinness in town. A large screen beams Sky Sports TV, packing in punters three deep at the narrow bar counter. *Ul.Św.Krzyża 15.* ☎ *012/421-61-88. www.nicnowego.com. All trams to Old Town. Map p 113.*

★★★ **Paparazzi** OLD TOWN   The self-styled top cocktail spot in town, Paparazzi exudes an image of coolness. Neither snobby nor exclusive, Paparazzi simply purveys proper mixed drinks to an appreciative clientele—prices are not significantly higher than elsewhere in the Old Town. Imaginative domestic touches feature prominently—the Polish Martini of Absolut, Żubrówka, and Krupnik, the Krakow variety with Absolut, Wiśniówka, and fresh grapefruit. *Ul.Mikolajska 9.* ☎ *012/429-45-97. All trams to Old Town. Map p 113.*

★★★ **Propaganda** KAZIMIERZ   Although it's a well-worn concept, this hard-drinking, Communist-themed Kazimierz bar wears it well. People (mainly locals) don't come here to gawp and coo at the old signage, machines, and banners, they plot up around the crowded wooden interior to banter loudly and get drunk. A musical soundtrack of indie, punk, and metal attracts a mainly (but not exclusively) male clientele, who somehow keep the party going to shortly before the trams start running. *Ul.Miodowa 20.* ☎ *012/292-04-02. Tram 7, 9, 11, 13, 24: Miodowa. Map p 114.*

★★ **Ptiasek** KAZIMIERZ   Set away from the Plac Nowy action, the "Bird" is the perfect spot to read, check e-mails, or play chess by day, or enjoy a couple of quiet ones to start the evening off. Taps of Guinness, Tyskie, and Pilsner Urquell are provided for tranquil sipping, with little squares of apple cake for something to nibble on. There's a garden in summer. *Ul.Dajwór 3.* ☎ *012/431-03-41. www.ptiasek.eu. Tram 7, 9, 11, 13, 24: Miodowa. Map p 114.*

The bohemian Mleczarnia.

Up in Smoke

The classic Krakow experience of late-night fun in a smoky cellar is no more. As of 2011, falling into line with nearly everywhere else in western Europe, Poland has banned smoking in public places. The move followed years of debate, bringing into question health issues, concepts of civic freedom, and so on. The end result, though, is that if bar or club owners can't provide a separate, well-ventilated room for smokers, they can face a fine of up to 2,000 zł. Those caught smoking where they shouldn't be can also expect punishment, leveled at 500 zł per individual. So far, the ban has hardly affected the bar trade but longer-term results have yet to be assessed.

★★★ **Singer** KAZIMIERZ There's a strong case for naming Singer the best bar in town—and on the right night, way past midnight, it can be. Drinkers gather around tables made from old sewing machines in two dimly-lit rooms to create an atmosphere of conspiratorial chatter. The drink of choice is not beer—although you might spot a few stray stags chugging away—but Wiśniówka, the sticky, cherry-flavored vodka that the barman will magically produce from behind a secret curtain. *Ul.Estery 20.* 📞 *012/292-06-22. Tram 7, 9, 11, 13, 24: Miodowa. Map p 114.*

Clubs

Awaria OLD TOWN A varied agenda of DJs and live acts keeps the regulars entertained at this good-time venue. Under the slogan "Enough Is Never Enough," locals and expats sink standard beers, cocktails, and vodka shots around a bar decked out in Americana. Mistletoe hanging over the counter causes a few giggles. *Ul.Mikolajska 9.* 📞 *012/292-03-50. www.klubawaria.com. No cover. All trams to Old Town. Map p 113.*

★ **Błędne Kolo** OLD TOWN In a small hub of bars and clubs that also includes Rdza (p 120), the "Vicious

Circle" occupies an attractive site of an inner courtyard, balcony, and first-floor setting. This is made righteously messy by a loyal gang of young regulars entertained by reliably competent local DJs. *Ul.Bracka 4.* 📞 *0500/190-142. www.bledne kolo.pl. Cover varies. All trams to Old Town. Map p 113.*

★ **Boom Bar Rush** OLD TOWN In the same building as Cztery Pokoje (p 115), BBR is an intimate, late-opening cellar club, the perfect last stop before bed. Regular DJs spin R&B and hip-hop 6 nights of the week, theme nights as well, though room to dance is in pretty short supply. *Ul.Gołębia 6.* 📞 *012/429-39-74. www.boombarrush.com. Closed Mon. No cover. All trams to Old Town. Map p 113.*

★ **Cień** OLD TOWN The red-lit cellar is perhaps Krakow's best nightspot for house DJs. The "Shadow" attracts a fashionable young crowd—there's no dress code but hair gel helps—who enjoy the constant crush between the bare-brick walls. *Ul.Św.Jana 15.* 📞 *012/422-21-77. Cover varies. All trams to Old Town. Map p 113.*

★ **Club Clu** KAZIMIERZ On tourist-swamped Szeroka, lined with

Arts & Entertainment Best Bets

Best **Concert Acoustics**
★★★ Krakow Philharmonic, *Ul.Zwierzyniecka 1 (p 125)*

Best **Jazz Club**
★★ Harris Piano Jazz Bar, *Rynek Główny 28 (p 127)*

Best **Opera House**
★★ Krakow Opera, *Ul.Lubicz 48 (p 125)*

Best **Music Festival**
★★ Sacrum Profanum, *(See Savvy Traveler, Festivals & Special Events, p 165)*

Best **Sports Entertainment**
★★ Wisła Krakow, *Ul Reymonta 22 (p 129)*

Best **Theater Performances**
★★★ Stary Theater, *Ul.Jagellońska 5 (p 130)*

Best **Theater Shows for Kids**
★★★ Groteska Theater, *Ul.Skarbowa 2 (p 130)*

Best **All-Around Venue**
★★ Showtime, *Rynek Główny 28 (p 129)*

Best **Live Music Venue**
★ Forty Kleparz, *Ul.Kamienna 2–4 (p 128)*

Best **All-Around Performance Venue**
★★★ Juliusz Słowacki Theater, *Pl.Św.Ducha 1 (p 125)*

Best **Classic Cinemas**
★★★ ARS Cinema, *Ul.Św.Jana 6 (p 125)*; ★★★ Pod Baranami, *Rynek Główny 27 (p 126)*

Best **Big Movie Screens**
★ Orange IMAX Krakow, *Al.Pokoju 44 (p 126)*; ★★ Kijów, *Ul.Krasińskiego 34 (p 126)*

Best **Grunge Den**
★★ Kawiarnia Naukowa, *Ul.Jakuba 29–31 (p 128)*

Best **Eclectic Music Agenda**
★★ Rotunda, *Ul.Oleandry 1 (p 128)*

Below: Kawiarnia Naukowa. Previous page: Juliusz Słowacki Theater.

Old Town A&E

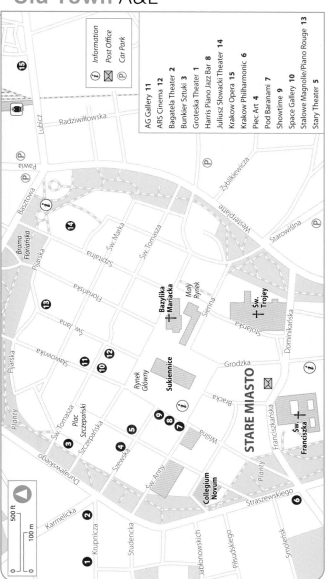

Information
Post Office
Car Park

AG Gallery 11
ARS Cinema 12
Bagatela Theater 2
Bunkier Sztuki 3
Groteska Theater 1
Harris Piano Jazz Bar 8
Juliusz Słowacki Theater 14
Krakow Opera 15
Krakow Philharmonic 6
Piec Art 4
Pod Baranami 7
Showtime 9
Space Gallery 10
Stalowe Magnolie/Piano Rouge 13
Stary Theater 5

Around Krakow A&E

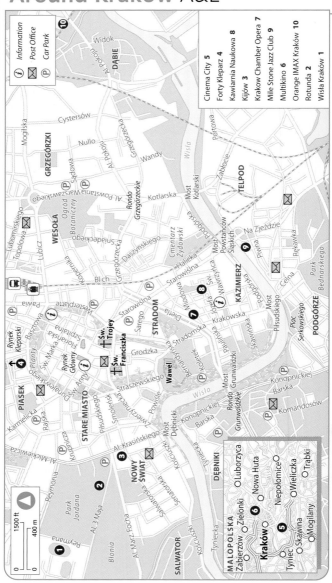

Cinema City **5**
Forty Kleparz **4**
Kawiarnia Naukowa **8**
Kijów **3**
Krakow Chamber Opera **7**
Mile Stone Jazz Club **9**
Multikino **6**
Orange IMAX Kraków **10**
Rotunda **2**
Wisła Kraków **1**

ⓘ Information
☒ Post Office
ⓟ Car Park

Arts & Entertainment **A to Z**

Classical Music & Opera

★★★ Juliusz Słowacki Theater

OLD TOWN   Krakow's most prestigious concert venue, an ornate confection at the northern end of Szpitalna dating from the 1890s, stages classical music, dance, and theater productions. It is most famous for having been the venue where Stanisław Wyspiański's seminal *Wesele* was premiered. The recent home of Krakow Opera while a new venue was being built on nearby Ulica Lubicz, the theater is named after the Polish dramatist and Romantic poet who died in exile in Paris in 1849. Concertgoers today can enjoy a pre-show drink at the stylish Café Trema downstairs. *Pl.Św.Ducha 1.* ☎ *012/424-45-00. www.slowacki.krakow.pl. Ticket prices vary. All trams to Dworzed Główny. Map p 123.*

★★ Krakow Chamber Opera

KAZIMIERZ   This intimate venue opened in 1991 thanks to actress and choreographer Jadwiga Leśniak-Jankowska. The Krakow Chamber Opera has been based here for most of the decade, its repertoire

Juliusz Słowacki Theater.

concentrating on old Polish traditional themes. *Ul.Miodowa 15.* ☎ *012/430-66-06. www.kok.art.pl. Ticket prices vary. Tram 7, 9, 11, 13, 24: Miodowa. Map p 124.*

★★ Krakow Opera

NEAR OLD TOWN   After a wait of 5 decades, a new, purpose-built Krakow Opera was unveiled in December 2008. Construction had been agreed in 2002 and a locally born architect, Romuald Loegler, had been commissioned. Responsible for a notably radical design job on the Łódz Philharmonic, Loegler devised a main stage with a computer-controlled acoustic ceiling and an equally movable orchestra pit. Smaller shows could be produced on the Na Antresoli stage or Chamber stage, while there was also room for a lecture hall, an exhibition space, and a restaurant. At last Krakow has the opera house it deserves. *Ul.Lubicz 48.* ☎ *012/296-61-00. www.opera. krakow.pl. Ticket prices vary. All trams to Lubicz. Map p 123.*

★★★ Krakow Philharmonic

NOWY ŚWIAT   This impressive neo-baroque pile, built in 1931, became the home of the then newly formed Krakow Philharmonic in the last days of the war in 1945. Its main auditorium has hosted many top international names, partly thanks to the involvement of Tadeusz Strugała as general and artistic director. Strugała, artistic director and chief conductor here in the 1980s, worked with Roman Polański on Oscar-winning film *The Pianist* in 2001. The current managing and artistic director is conductor Paweł Przytocki. The Philharmonic also contains two rooms for chamber concerts. *Ul.Zwierzyniecka 1.* ☎ *012/422-94-77. www.filharmonia.krakow.pl.*

Ticket prices vary. All trams to Filharmonia. Map p 123.

Film

★★★ ARS Cinema OLD TOWN
The most elegant cinema in Krakow, set in two historic mansions a short walk from the main market square, comprises five screening rooms. An adventurous agenda of European and arthouse works forms the bulk of the repertoire, while popular family-friendly films also get a look-in. *Ul.Św.Jana 6.* ☎ *012/421-41-99. www.ars.pl. Ticket prices vary. All trams to Old Town. Map p 123.*

★ Cinema City ŁAGIEWNIKI
Set on the main road leading south from the city center an easy tram ride away, this 10-screen complex is the most comfortable venue to enjoy a movie in Krakow. Great for sound and special effects, Cinema City also scores high for accommodating wheelchair-bound moviegoers. It now has three other branches in town, including a new one at the Bonarka City Center (p 79). *Ul.Zakopiańska 62.* ☎ *012/295-95-00. www.cinemacity.pl. Ticket prices vary. Trams 8, 19, 22, 23, 40: Solvay. Map p 124.*

★★ Kijów NOWY ŚWIAT
A major venue for the Krakow Film Festival,

The contemporary Kijów cinema.

the contemporary Kijów can boast the largest cinema screen in central Krakow. As well as the 800-seater Large Hall, the Kijów also screens movies in an intimate studio space. The venue celebrated its 40th anniversary in 2007 by opening a basement DJ club accessed through the lobby. Kijów also houses an excellent cafe-bar for pre- and post-film drinks. *Ul.Krasińskiego 34.* ☎ *012/433-00-33. www.kijow.pl. Ticket prices vary. All trams to Cracovia. Map p 124.*

★ Multikino N.E. KRAKOW
This huge multiplex stands north of the city center, conveniently right by the Aqua Park. A dozen screening rooms show mainly standard Hollywood fare, with regular all-night themed marathons also programmed. The three bars include one especially for sports fans. *Ul.Dobrego Pasterza 128.* ☎ *012/376-43-10. www.multikino.pl. All buses to Dobrego Pasztorza. Ticket prices vary. Map p 124.*

★ Orange IMAX Kraków
DĄBIE Wildlife, sci-fi, and adventure features are brought to life on the vast screen here. The venue is an easy hop on the tram from town, heading toward Nowa Huta. *Krakow Plaza, Al.Pokoju 44.* ☎ *012/290-90-90. www.kinoimax.pl. Ticket prices vary. Trams 1, 14, 22: Krakow Plaza, Map p 124.*

★★★ Pod Baranami OLD TOWN
Right on the main market square, this palatial arena is one of the most famous cultural institutions in Krakow. The cinema comprises three screening rooms, showing classic European and arthouse films. *Rynek Główny 27.* ☎ *012/423-07-68. www.kinopodbaranami.pl. Ticket prices vary. All trams to Old Town. Map p 123.*

Jazz & Cabaret

★★ Harris Piano Jazz Bar OLD TOWN   Right on the market square, this basement club is one of Krakow's most popular music venues. All the big names in Polish jazz have played here. The regular appearance of foreign guests and a flexible music policy—blues, R&B, and folk—mean that Harris fills in summer and winter. It's opening until 2am and serves a selection of 20 cocktails from a long, busy bar counter to keep the party going. *Rynek Główny 28.* ☎ *012/421-57-41. www.harris.krakow.pl. Cover varies. All trams to Old Town. Map p 123.*

Harris Piano Jazz Bar.

Mile Stone Jazz Club PODGÓRZE   With its luxurious settees and low lighting, the Mile Stone on the ground floor of the Qubus Hotel is just the right place for a posh date—the discerning jazz fan is unlikely to find anything cutting-edge on stage here. A gentle agenda of swing and modern sounds is lined up for weekends. The riverside location lends a relaxing tone to the evening. *Qubus Hotel, Ul.Nadwiślańska 6.* ☎ *012/ 374-51-86. www.mile-stone.pl. No cover. All trams to Pl.Bohaterów Getta. Map p 124.*

★★ Piec Art OLD TOWN   Opened in 1999, this downtown jazz club has attracted all the great Polish names thanks to its central location and renowned acoustics—the venue bills itself as the "Acoustic Jazz Club." With its high-ceilinged interior and superior catering, it attracts the more well-heeled jazz aficionado, and is priced accordingly. *Ul.Szewska 12.* ☎ *012/429-64-25. www.piecart. pl. Cover varies. All trams to Old Town. Map p 123.*

Advance Tickets & Listings

For the latest concert, theater, and event listings, pick up a copy of the monthly *Karnet* (http://en.karnet.krakow.pl), as well as a bimonthly **events guide,** both widely available. The website www. krakow-info.com/events.htm has a day-by-day breakdown of local shows in every genre. For exhibitions and general events around town, especially for children, the pocket-sized **kurs na kurs** (www. kursnakurs.pl) is handy, although Polish-language only.

The people behind Karnet are linked with the **Krakow Info** points across town, where you can buy tickets for (mainly) classical performances—see www.en.infokrakow.pl for details. For music festivals and the bigger rock shows, your best bet is **Empik** (Rynek Główny 5, ☎ **012/423-81-90,** www.empik.com) on the main square.

Krakow Film Festival

Celebrating its 50th anniversary in 2011, the Krakow Film Festival is one of Europe's most prestigious. Taking place in late May, with the **Kijów cinema** (p 126) as its main venue, over 7 days the KFF focuses on documentary, short, and animated films. All in all, some 250 works are shown, Polish and international, the organizers having decided to invite domestic and global filmmakers as part of its 40th anniversary celebrations in 2001. While the Polish film industry suffered the upheavals of the 1990s, the festival raised its profile by having key arthouse directors appear, such as Mike Leigh and Werner Herzog. Before this, Krakow promoted the work of little-known domestic documentary makers and animators, notably Krzysztof Kieślowski, who got an early break here. In 2007 the KFF incorporated feature-length films, the top director awarded the Golden Horn. See www.kff.com.pl.

★★★ **Stalowe Magnolie/Piano Rouge** OLD TOWN   These two, mainly jazz venues under the same management share a similar scarlet color scheme and louche style. Sister establishment the Piano Rouge (Rynek Główny 46) sits on the main square—jazz piano sets suit the atmosphere perfectly. The "Steel Magnolias" has a long-established reputation hosting quality local jazz trios and solo singers. Expect a cover charge for men and steep drinks prices. *Ul.Św.Jana 15.* ☎ *012/422-84-72. www.stalowemagnolie.com. Cover (men only) 15 zł. All trams to Old Town. Map p 123.*

Pop & Rock

★ **Forty Kleparz** NEAR OLD TOWN   Despite, or perhaps because of, an unfashionable location toward Kleparz market north of the Old Town, this atmospheric spot has established itself as one of the main venues for live music in town. Making good use of Kleparz Fort, a former Habsburg bastion, and with a decent sound system, it is equally as adept at staging top (mainly) Polish bands as top Polish DJs. *Ul.Kamienna 2–4.* ☎ *606/388-313. www.fortykleparz.com. Closed Mon–Wed, Sun. Cover varies. Trams 3: Nowy Kleparz. Map p 124.*

★★ **Kawiarnia Naukowa** KAZIM-IERZ   Krakow's main grunge bar stages the occasional live act in a cramped side room. Even if there's not a band on, the vinyl spun behind the big stone bar is worth a visit to darkest Kazimierz—punk, Johnny Cash, Nirvana, whatever. Wonderfully friendly bar staff serves a loyal clientele. *Ul.Jakuba 29–31.* ☎ *663/83-34-57. www.kawiarnianaukowa. ovh.org. No cover. Tram 7, 9, 11, 13, 24: Miodowa. Map p 124.*

★★ **Rotunda** CZARNA WIES   Many a band has trodden the boards at this student-center venue near Park Jordan, a couple of tram stops from the Old Town. The booking policy is completely random—rock, rap, indie from home and abroad—but you might also find classical, spoken word, or an evening with the local mountaineering

Kawiarnia Naukowa.

society. *Ul.Oleandry 1.* ☎ *012/292-65-16. www.rotunda.pl. Cover varies. Trams 15, 18: Oleandry. Map p 124.*

★★ **Showtime** OLD TOWN   Right on the market square, this bohemian space hosts live music of all genres—anything that fits onto its modest stage, in fact. One floor up, this is a rare Rynek Główny venue with a view of the square from above. Scale the carpeted staircase lined with bizarre decorations and see what's on that night. *Rynek Główny 28.* ☎ *012/421-47-14. www. showtimeclub.pl. No cover. All trams to Old Town. Map p 123.*

Spectator Sports
★★ **Wisła Kraków** CZARNA WIES   Poland's top soccer team in recent years play at the best league ground in the country. Despite this, and the city's palpably obvious talent for tourism, Krakow inexplicably missed out

Local Galleries

To check out the art scene in Krakow, you should head to the **Bunkier Sztuki** (Pl.Szczepański 3a, ☎ **012/422-40-21,** http://bunkier. art.pl). This Modernist building on the Planty houses some of the city's best contemporary art exhibitions. As well as regular thought-provoking, mainly Polish shows, the "Art Bunker" hosts World Press Photo exhibitions in the fall. One of the first private galleries to open in Krakow, the **Space Gallery** (Ul.Św.Marka 7, ☎ **012/432-29-20,** www. spacegallery.com.pl) was set up by sculptress Barbara Zambrzycka-Śliwa. Beginning with the 19th century (Matejko, the Paris School), it works its way up to regularly changing works of the modern day on the upper floor. Also in the Old Town, the **AG Gallery** (Pl.Dominikański 2, ☎ **602/686-622,** www.galeriaag.art.pl) hosts works by Poland's most outstanding contemporary artists. The in-house collection is constantly being added to.

Bagatela Theater for light comedy and musicals.

on hosting the Euro2012 championships. This, despite the fact that the now modern stadium by the Park Jordana has had its capacity doubled to 33,000. In the meantime, the home team plays every other weekend between August and May. Check the website for times—tickets can be bought on the day. Prestigious European games are an annual event—visitors have included Barcelona and Real Madrid. *Ul.Reymonta 22.* ☎ *012/630-76-00. www.wisla.krakow.pl. Ticket prices vary. Trams 15, 18: Reymana n/z. Map p 124.*

Theater
★★★ Bagatela Theater NEAR OLD TOWN
Founded in 1919, the Bagatela occupies an impressive building where Karmelicka meets Krupnicza. Known for its light comedies and musicals, the Bagatela is also named after poet and literary professor Tadeusz Boy-Żeleński, murdered in the war. *Ul.Karmelicka 6.* ☎ *012/424-52-00. www.bagatela.pl. Ticket prices vary. All trams to Teatr Bagatela. Map p 123.*

★★★ Groteska Theater NEAR OLD TOWN
Based at this remarkable building in the University Quarter since 1945, the Groteska also stages open-air puppet shows and re-enactments of Polish fairy tales in the main market square in summer. During the fall–spring season, the Groteska produces mask and costume dramas for children and adults, some veering to the experimental side. Children's workshops are also held. *Ul.Skarbowa 2.* ☎ *012/633-48-22. www.groteska.pl. Ticket prices vary. All trams to Old Town. Map p 123.*

★★★ Stary Theater OLD TOWN
Krakow's "Old Theater" has reflected the monumental changes in Polish history over its 200-plus years. Founded in 1781, and based at this building since 1799, the Stary had its heyday with the great names of the 19th century. Closed in the early 1900s, the Stary reopened immediately after the war, only for each subsequent director to come to loggerheads with the government censor. Much is documented in the modest museum downstairs, where you'll also find the **Maska cafe,** done out in the same Art Nouveau style as the theater's facade. The Stary stages both Polish and international productions. *Ul.Jagellońska 5.* ☎ *012/422-85-66. www.stary-teatr. pl. Ticket prices vary. All trams to Old Town. Map p 123.* ●

Puppet from the Groteska Theater.

Lodging Best Bets

Best Romantic Hotels
★★★ Gródek, *Ul.na Gródku 4* (p 139); ★★★ Amadeus, *Ul.Mikolajska 20 (p 135)*

Best Panoramic Pool
★★★ Qubus Hotel, *Ul.Nadwiślańska 6 (p 143)*

Best Historic Conversions
★★★ Copernicus, *Ul.Kanonicza 16* (p 136); ★★★ Pugetów, *Ul.Starowiślna 15a (p 143)*

Best Riverside Views
★ Poleski, *Ul.Sandomierska 6 (p 142)*

Best Art Nouveau Decor
★ Pollera, *Ul.Szpitalna 30 (p 143)*

Best on the Main Market Square
★★★ Wentzl, *Rynek Główny 19* (p 146); ★★★ Pałac Bonerowski, *Ul.Św.Jana 1 (p 141)*

Best Surprising Attractions
★★ Eden, *Ul.Ciemna 15 (p 137)*

Best Spa Hotel
★★★ Farmona Business Hotel & Spa, *Ul.Jugowicka 10c (p 137)*

Best for Backpackers
★★ Good Bye Lenin, *Ul.Grodzka 34* (p 138)

Best Film-Set Location
★★★ Grand Hotel, *Ul.Sławkowska 5–7 (p 138)*

Best Bed & Breakfast
★★ Kolory Bed & Breakfast, *Ul.Estery 10 (p 140)*

Best Kazimierz Lodging
★★ Rubinstein, *Ul.Szeroka 12* (p 144)

Best Family Hotel
★ Novotel Krakow Centrum, *Ul.Kościuszki 5 (p 141)*

Best for Visiting Wawel
★ Pod Wawelem, *Pl.Na Groblach 22a (p 142)*; ★★ Sheraton Krakow, *Ul.Powiśle 7 (p 144)*

Best Wawel Views
★★ Kossak, *Pl.Kossaka 1 (p 140)*

Below: Wentzl, one of the best market square locations. Previous page: Ostoya Palace Hotel.

Old Town Lodging

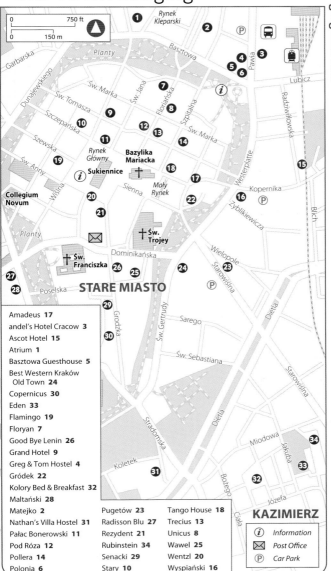

Amadeus **17**
andel's Hotel Cracow **3**
Ascot Hotel **15**
Atrium **1**
Basztowa Guesthouse **5**
Best Western Kraków
  Old Town **24**
Copernicus **30**
Eden **33**
Flamingo **19**
Floryan **7**
Good Bye Lenin **26**
Grand Hotel **9**
Greg & Tom Hostel **4**
Gródek **22**
Kolory Bed & Breakfast **32**
Maltański **28**
Matejko **2**
Nathan's Villa Hostel **31**
Pałac Bonerowski **11**
Pod Róza **12**
Pollera **14**
Polonia **6**

Pugetów **23**
Radisson Blu **27**
Rezydent **21**
Rubinstein **34**
Senacki **29**
Stary **10**

Tango House **18**
Trecius **13**
Unicus **8**
Wawel **25**
Wentzl **20**
Wyspiański **16**

i Information
⊠ Post Office
Ⓟ Car Park

Kazimierz & Podgórze Lodging

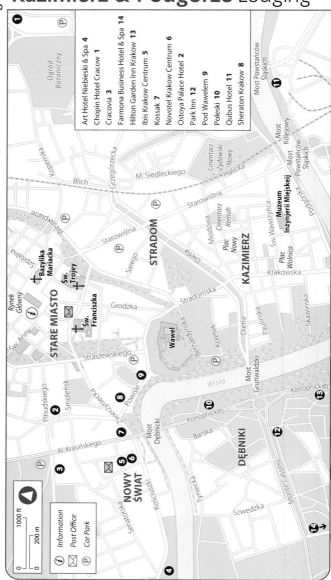

Art Hotel Niebieski & Spa **4**
Chopin Hotel Cracow **1**
Cracovia **3**
Farmona Business Hotel & Spa **14**
Hilton Garden Inn Krakow **13**
Ibis Krakow Centrum **5**
Kossak **7**
Novotel Krakow Centrum **6**
Ostoya Palace Hotel **2**
Park Inn **12**
Pod Wawelem **9**
Poleski **10**
Qubus Hotel **11**
Sheraton Krakow **8**

i Information
⊠ Post Office
Ⓟ Car Park

1000 ft
200 m

Krakow **Lodging A to Z**

★★★ **Amadeus** OLD TOWN This converted 16th-century town house is one of Krakow's most opulent hotels, popular with visiting writers and classical pianists. The title refers to the baroque style of the rooms and public spaces, including the cellar restaurant and cafe, purveyor of delicate little cakes. Amid all this chintz, the service is first-class, befitting Amadeus' four-star status. *Ul.Mikolajska 20.* ☎ *012/429-60-70. www.hotel-amadeus.pl. 24 units. Doubles 500 zł–800 zł. AE, DC, MC, V. All trams to Old Town. Map p 133.*

★★ **andel's Hotel Cracow** NEAR OLD TOWN Dominating the landscaped square by the train station, this sleek business hotel allows for a comfortable, quiet, high-tech stay. Flatscreen TVs, high-speed Internet, and under-floor heated bathrooms feature throughout, with gym, sauna, and massage treatments also available. Guests mingle in Oscar's Bar and the Delight restaurant with its summer terrace. *Ul.Pawia 3.* ☎ *012/660-01-00. www.andels cracow.com. 159 units. Doubles 375 zł–900 zł. AE, DC, MC, V. All trams to Dworzec Główny. Map p 133.*

★ **Art Hotel Niebieski & Spa** SALWATOR This contemporary, five-star establishment by the Salwator tram terminus offers quality comfort within an easy hop of the city center. With a recommendable modern terrace restaurant, Vanilla Sky (p 108), and superb spa, the Niebieski also gets the basics right, with light, fashionable guest rooms, large beds, and floor-heated bathrooms. Finally, breakfast is absolutely divine, a wide choice of Polish delights taken above the Vistula waterfront. *Ul.Flisacka 3.* ☎ *012/ 297-40-40. www.niebieski.com.pl. 40*

andel's Hotel Cracow is popular with business travelers.

units. Doubles 450 zł–550 zł. AE, DC, MC, V. Trams 1, 2, 6: Salwator Pętla. Map p 134.

Ascot Hotel NEAR OLD TOWN Opened in 2007 near the main train station, east of the Old Town, this modern, comfortable three-star is a handy mid-range option close to the action. Free wireless Internet comes in all rooms along with a white, orange, and pastel color scheme, also used in the public spaces— both bar and restaurant have a contemporary feel. *Ul.Radwiłałowska 3.* ☎ *012/384-06-06. www.ascothotel. pl. 49 units. Doubles 300 zł–360 zł. AE, DC, MC, V. All trams to Lubicz. Map p 133.*

★ **Atrium** NEAR OLD TOWN Only a three-star, but Atrium is perfectly comfortable and set in a quiet location north of the Old Town near Kleparz market. The neat rooms and

The Best Lodging

restaurant exude light and space, all equipped with modern furnishings and ably manned by a polite staff. Discounts are offered on room rates and meals in summer. *Ul.Krzywa 7.* ☎ *012/430-02-03. www.hotelatrium. com.pl. 52 units. Doubles 300 zł–335 zł. AE, DC, MC, V. All trams to Nowy Kleparz. Map p 133.*

★ **Basztowa Guesthouse** NEAR OLD TOWN A centrally located bargain just a hop from the main train station. Rooms with their own shower are nearly twice the price of those without—these showers being rather compact, the outlay is hardly worth it. No complaints with the rest of the furnishings, the style of this 19th-century town house brought out by the carved woods and parquet floors. Pick up your keys from the Hotel Polonia next door. *Ul.Basztowa 24.* ☎ *012/429-51-81. www.hotel sinkrakow.pl. 26 units. Doubles 150 zł. AE, DC, MC, V. All trams to Dworzec Główny. Map p 133.*

Best Western Kraków Old Town NEAR OLD TOWN Part of the Best Western group, this is a comfortable, mid-range, city-center lodging to match any in town in the same price bracket. The classic rooms here are pretty basic, so for a more luxurious stay, opt for a 'Lux'

room featuring retro-style chairs, bold stripes and plenty of space to relax. A standard range of services (laundry, tour booking, parking) is provided by a friendly staff—another pleasant change from the bad old days. *Ul.Św.Gertrudy 6.* ☎ *012/422-76-66. www.bwkrakow.pl. 91 units. Doubles 319 zł–489 zł. AE, DC, MC, V. All trams to Św.Gertrudy. Map p 133.*

★ **Chopin Hotel Cracow** GRZE-GORZKI Three-star sister of the andel's Hotel Cracow (p 135), the Chopin is equally bright and breezy if perhaps a tad more functional than its more prestigious relation. Set just east of the Old Town, a couple of tram stops away from its stablemate, it offers guests just enough attractions (bar, restaurant, gym, massage treatments, salon, summer garden) that those here on short stays needn't go into town at all. All rooms have free high-speed Wi-Fi too. *Ul.Przy Rondzie 2.* ☎ *012/299-00-00. www.chopinhotel.com. 219 units. Doubles 215 zł–275 zł. AE, DC, MC, V. All trams to Rondo Mogilskie. Map p 134.*

★★★ **Copernicus** OLD TOWN Candidate for best lodging in town, Poland's only Relais & Châteaux hotel is both historic (it's an early 16th-century conversion) and

Art Hotel Niebieski & Spa.

Copernicus, the hotel favored by visiting royals and presidents.

contemporary (high-speed Wi-Fi in each room). Designers have, somehow, arranged a swimming pool, gym, and sauna in the medieval cellars. The sumptuous furnishings fit the surroundings, and the restaurant is one of Krakow's finest. *Ul.Kanonicza 16.* ☎ *012/424-34-00. www.hotel.com.pl. 29 units. Doubles 900 zł–980 zł. AE, DC, MC, V. All trams to Old Town. Map p 133.*

★ **Cracovia** NEAR OLD TOWN Handy for the National Museum and soccer grounds, the Cracovia is the setting-off point for tourist buses to Auschwitz, Wieliczka, and beyond. The rooms are pretty functional but improved of late, with Internet access and direct-dial international telephone lines. Canoeing, horse-riding, tennis, cycling, and swimming can be organized for an extra fee. *Al.Focha 1.* ☎ *012/424-56-00. www.accorhotels.com. 314 units. Doubles 165 zł–400 zł. AE, DC, MC, V. All trams to Cracovia. Map p 134.*

★★ **Eden** KAZIMIERZ This otherwise modest hotel in the Jewish quarter hides a surprising array of unusual facilities, most notably the only authentic mikvah bath in town. The other unexpected feature is a salt grotto, while a sauna and

massage are also available on-site (at an extra cost). Also to hand is a genuinely kosher restaurant and a sports bar, in a historic part of a building once occupied by Isaac Jakubowicz, founder of the nearby synagogue of the same name. *Ul.Ciemna 15.* ☎ *012/430-65-65. www.hoteleden.pl. 27 units. Doubles 240 zł–260 zł. AE, DC, MC, V. Tram 7, 9, 11, 13, 24: Miodowa. Map p 133.*

★★★ **Farmona Business Hotel & Spa** LAGIEWNIKI This wonderful leafy retreat is worth the hassle of its out-of-town location. Set in an extensive garden with gazebo, the Farmona provides the finest spa treatments in Krakow and the best hotel breakfast, served on the terrace of the Restaurant Magnifica, whose fusion cuisine alone warrants an evening here. The steam room and dry sauna (watch out for the weird jungle sounds) can be enjoyed with a range of treatments. *Ul.Jugowicka 10c.* ☎ *012/252-70-70. www.farmonahotel.com. 31 units. Doubles 329 zł–369 zł. AE, DC, MC, V. Bus 104. Map p 134.*

★★ **Flamingo** OLD TOWN There are currently about a hundred hostels in Krakow—when this superior one set up a few years ago near the

Flamingo hostel for a great base in the Old Town.

main square, there were 30. Despite this, the Flamingo beats its competitors, and not just because of location. Some 50 guests are catered for with a kitchen, laundry, comfortable common room with TV, two free Internet terminals, and clean, modern bathrooms. They are also entertained with regular events. Reception is 24 hours and the management also runs a number of comfortable apartments in Floriańska. *Ul.Szewska 4. ☎ 012/422-00-00. www.flamingo-hostel.com. 12 units/54 beds. Dorm beds (max 10 to a room) from 40 zł. Doubles 80 zł–90 zł. AE, DC, MC, V. All trams to Old Town. Map p 133.*

★ **Floryan** OLD TOWN   What the Floryan lacks in add-ons it makes up for with location, near the Floriańska Gate, a 5-minute walk from the main square. Thanks to some inventive shopping at Ikea, the rooms are surprisingly comfortable, considering this is a 16th-century building—the medieval cellar now housing the Vesuvio restaurant and its wood-fire pizza oven has been used as a hostelry for centuries. The lobby is where you book for Crazy Guides' tours of Nowa Huta (p 65). *Ul.Floriańska 38. ☎ 012/431-14-18. www.floryan.com.pl. 21 units. Doubles 320 zł–430 zł. AE, DC, MC, V. All trams to Old Town. Map p 133.*

★★ **Good Bye Lenin** OLD TOWN Trading on laughing at Poland's now distant Communist history, Good Bye Lenin offers an excellent hostel service and funny decorative touches to keep the joke going. Plus points include towels, free Wi-Fi, a decent buffet breakfast spread, and use of spacious lockers. If this place, a short walk from the main square, is full, then there's another branch at Joselewicza 23 on the northern fringes of Kazimierz. *Ul.Grodzka 34. ☎ 012/430-30-53. www.goodbye lenin.pl. 8 units/46 beds. Dorm beds*

30 zł. Doubles 80 zł–90 zł. AE, DC, MC, V. All trams to Old Town. Map p 133.

★★★ **Grand Hotel** OLD TOWN Grand in terms of history and appearance, this venerable establishment was converted from the Czartoryski Palace in the late 19th century into the most luxurious hotel in the region. Occupied by the Nazis and left to decay afterwards, the Grand is now restored to its former glory. The rooms echo the decor of the late 1800s, while suites contain some original furniture and detailing. The lobby and other public areas attract a classy clientele and film crews—this was the first hotel in town to gain a five-star status. Pop in for a Viennese coffee or look for cheaper rates in quieter periods. *Ul.Sławkowska 5–7. ☎ 012/424-08-00. www.grand.pl. 64 units. Doubles 400 zł–1,100 zł. AE, DC, MC, V. All trams to Old Town. Map p 133.*

★ **Greg & Tom Hostel** NEAR OLD TOWN   This award-winning hostel near the train station suits the short- and long-term visitor alike. Spacious dorm rooms, breakfast until 11am, kitchen facilities, laundry, two free Internet terminals—Greg & Tom has come a long way since a modest

Grand Hotel.

The folksy Kolory, above Les Couleurs.

house of 12 beds was opened in 2004. Now it can offer three new double rooms, and extra accommodations in the Old Town to deal with the overflow. Stag parties are not welcome—otherwise, this is as hospitable and as convivial as it gets for the price. *Ul.Pawia 12/7.* ☎ *012/422-41-00. www.gregtomhostel.com. 15 units/23 beds. Dorm beds 55 zł–70 zł. Doubles 140 zł–170 zł. AE, DC, MC, V. All trams to Dworzec Główny. Map p 133.*

★★★ **Gródek** OLD TOWN A boutique hotel in the Donimirski group, this property dates back to the 11th century. Once the residence of the Tarnowski family, then part of the Dominican convent, the building feels solid and historic. The medieval clay pots, figures, and tiles unearthed with the hotel conversion in 2004 are on display in the restaurant downstairs, where a superior breakfast is served until mid-morning. All rooms have heated bathroom floors and tend to get smarter and pricier as you ascend, until you reach a lovely roof terrace open to all. There is also a cluster of three that can be blocked off and hired as a family suite. *Ul.na Gródku 4.* ☎ *012/431-90-30. www.donimirski. com. 23 units. Doubles 440 zł–670 zł. AE, DC, MC, V. All trams to Old Town. Map p 133.*

★ **Hilton Garden Inn Krakow** DĘBNIKI Krakow's latest luxury hotel is Poland's first Hilton Garden Inn, and takes full advantage of the under-used land facing Wawel from just over the river. The HGI offers expansive rooms, a gym, bar, and restaurant, and handy conveniences such as a coin laundry, 24-hour food outlet, and well-appointed business center. Video conferencing is also on hand. *Ul.Marii Konopnickiej 33.* ☎ *012/399-90-00. www.hgi.com. 154 units. Doubles 1,270 zł–1,650 zł. AE, DC, MC, V. All trams to Most Grunwaldzki. Map p 134.*

★ **Ibis Krakow Centrum** NOWY ŚWIAT All rooms and public areas have been renovated at this French chain hotel, so breakfast (from 4am), a drink, or a meal at the terrace L'Estaminet is a comfortable pleasure rather than a cramped necessity. The location is great too, right by the river, within easy reach of Wawel, Kazimierz, and the Old Town. All rooms have flatscreen TVs, free Internet access, and nice big beds, and you can call up room service for snacks 24 hours a day. *Ul.Syrkomil 2.* ☎ *012/299-33-00. www.accorhotels.com. 175 units. Doubles 199 zł–229 zł. AE, DC, MC, V. All trams to Jubilat. Map p 134.*

★★ Kolory Bed & Breakfast

KAZIMIERZ Thirteen spacious rooms, well furnished with folksy designs and artifacts, are set above Les Couleurs cafe (p 116), right on Plac Nowy, the heart of everything that's happening in Kazimierz. Breakfast—fresh, fluffy croissants, decent coffee, and fruit juice—is taken downstairs, where you can check e-mails, although there is also Internet access in your room. Each room also has its own ensuite bathroom, satellite TV, and air-conditioning. *Ul.Estery 10.* ☎ *012/421-04-65. www.kolory.com.pl. 13 units. Doubles 190 zł–230 zł. AE, DC, MC, V. Tram 7, 9, 11, 13, 24: Miodowa. Map p 133.*

★★ Kossak NEAR OLD TOWN

This impressive new four-star opened in the spring of 2011, making use of a prime position just west of the Old Town. The location offers the bulk of the comfortable, tastefully furnished rooms an enviable view of Wawel. All have light color schemes, spacious bathrooms, and individually controlled air-conditioning. Notable features include the contemporary Percheron and the Oranżeria cafe with its panoramic terrace. *Pl.Kossaka 1.* ☎ *012/379-59-00. www.hotelkossak.pl. 60 units.*

Doubles 540 zł–580 zł. AE, DC, MC, V. All trams to Jubilat. Map p 134.

★★ Maltański NEAR OLD TOWN

The "Maltese" was the first of the historic buildings of the boutique Donimirski group to be converted into a hotel in 2000 and looks as classy now as it did then. The tiled floors, original art in each guest room, and a leafy terrace where breakfast is taken in warmer months makes this an alluring three-star stay. The usual Donimirski touches are also provided, such as free Internet access, heated bathroom floors, and fluffy bathrobes. *Ul.Straszewskiego 14.* ☎ *012/431-00-10. www.donimirski.com. 16 units. Doubles 430 zł–570 zł. AE, DC, MC, V. All trams to Filharmonia. Map p 133.*

Matejko NEAR OLD TOWN

Facilities, furnishings, and services have all been significantly improved at this pretty town house just outside the Old Town. Laundry, sauna, and massage can now all be provided, while guest rooms are bright and comfortably furnished. A bar, beer garden, and restaurant make for one of the nicest and most convenient three-star stays in town. *Pl.Matejki 8.* ☎ *012/422-47-37. www.matejkohotel.pl. 48 units. Doubles 320 zł–420 zł. AE, DC,*

Best Western Kraków Old Town (see review p 136).

The converted 19th-century Ostoya Palace Hotel.

MC, V. All trams to Basztowa LOT. Map p 133.

★ Nathan's Villa Hostel STRA-DOM
Between the southern fringe of the city center and the northern edge of Kazimierz, this is one of Krakow's most attractive hostels, offering an impressive array of free services. Complimentary laundry is a huge boon for the passing backpacker, but those staying a little longer can take advantage of the ping-pong and pool tables, a movie lounge, varied events nights, Wi-Fi, and the fully-fitted kitchen. The clean bathrooms are equipped with powerful showers, better than in most three-star hotels. Dorm beds range from 42 zł to 62 zł. depending on the time of year. Ul.Św.Agnieszki 1. ☎ 012/422-35-45. www.nathans villa.com. 21 units/114 dorm beds. Doubles 160 zł–180 zł. AE, DC, MC, V. All trams to Stradom. Map p 133.

★ Novotel Krakow Centrum
NOWY ŚWIAT   Near its French-chain sister, the Ibis Centrum, this well-facilitated riverside hotel suits business traveler and family alike. A pool, Jacuzzi, gym, sauna, and play-room all open from early in the day, and video games are available in each of the bright and neatly furnished rooms. Brasserie and bar are equally bright and light-filled, while some rooms on the upper floors have great views of Wawel Castle just the other side of a bend in the river. Ul.Kościuszki 5. ☎ 012/299-29-00. www.novotel.com. 198 units. Doubles 330 zł–675 zł. AE, DC, MC, V. All trams to Jubilat. Map p 134.

★ Ostoya Palace Hotel NEAR OLD TOWN
Another hotel conversion of a 19th-century palace, but all the same a welcome addition to accommodations options in the luxury bracket. Architect Józef Pokutyński's opulent Ostaszewski Palace was completed in 1895, but sadly allowed to lapse into decay after World War II. Its recent renovation has seen it transformed into 24 four-star rooms in soothing pastel colors, all with heated bathroom floors, some with separate tubs and showers. A sauna is also provided, while the bar, restaurant, and patio are done out in similar historic style. Ul.Piłsudskiego 24. ☎ 012/430-90-00. www.ostoyapalace.pl. 24 units. Doubles 380 zł–680 zł. AE, DC, MC, V. Tram 15, 18: Uniwersytet Jagielloński. Map p 134.

★★★ Pałac Bonerowski OLD TOWN
On the corner of the market square and Św.Jana, this historic five-star comprises eight standard rooms and six large suites, most featuring architectural detail installed as the property passed through various well-to-do families over the centuries. The most recent renovation came when the palace was converted into a hotel in 2005, the grand staircase and chandeliers now back in regular use. Contemporary additions—saunas, plasma TVs, broadband Internet—complement an unsurpassed view of the square. Note, also, the new Milano restaurant, lending the establishment a fresh profile. Ul.Św.Jana 1. ☎ 012/374-13-00. www.palacbonerowski.pl.

14 units. Doubles 630 zł–720 zł. AE, DC, MC, V. All trams to Old Town. Map p 133.

★ **Park Inn** DĘBNIKI Part of the Radisson family, this modern, stylish chain hotel occupies a huge area of undeveloped Dębniki. Part of a brightly logoed, urban brand that has expanded considerably across Europe after its launch on Berlin Alexanderplatz, Park Inns offer superb business facilities as well as comfort for the leisure traveler—and Krakow's is no exception. Here you'll also find a grill restaurant, spa, gym, and ample parking. *Ul.Monte Cassino 2.* ☎ *012/375-55-55. www. parkinn.com/hotel-krakow. 152 units. Doubles 400 zł–550 zł. AE, DC, MC, V. All trams to Most Grun-waldzki. Map p 134.*

★★ **Pod Róza** OLD TOWN Tsar Alexander I, Franz Liszt, and Honoré de Balzac have all passed through this grand doorway on Floriańska. Ornaments and textiles embellish the sense of grandeur and history, an atmosphere that extends to the first-class restaurant set over two floors in the lobby atrium, and to the cafe and the wine cellar. *Ul.Floriańska 14.* ☎ *012/424-33-00. www.hotel.com.pl. 57 units. Doubles 720 zł–750 zł. AE, DC, MC, V. All trams to Old Town. Map p 133.*

★ **Pod Wawelem** NEAR WAWEL Regularly featured as a cheap option on generic booking sites, 'Beneath Wawel' is a good find. Within a short walk of Wawel and the Old Town, and a pleasant riverside stroll from Kazimierz, the hotel offers water-front views from many of its tidy rooms. Guests are entitled to deals at the contemporary Malecon res-taurant, whose standard would more befit a four-star. Further ame-nities include a modest basement gym and sauna. *Pl.Na Groblach 22A.* ☎ *012/426-26-25. www.hotelpod wawelem.pl. 48 units. Doubles 170 zł–380 zł. AE, DC, MC, V. All trams to Jubilat. Map p 134.*

★ **Poleski** DĘBNIKI Opened in 2006, this is one of the few hotels in Krakow to make great use of a river-side location. Immediately opposite Wawel (rooms without a castle view are about 50 zł cheaper), the Poleski has a little-known restaurant whose continuous window seems to run the entire length of the Vistula. The rooms are on the comfortable side of functional, with standard fittings, but any sense of claustrophobia is alleviated by the top floor's pan-oramic terrace. *Ul.Sandomierska 6.* ☎ *012/260-54-05. www.hotel poleski.pl. 20 units. Doubles 225 zł–350 zł. AE, DC, MC, V. All trams to Most Grunwaldzki. Map p 134.*

Stained-glass Wyspiański windows at Pollera.

Radisson Blu.

★ **Pollera** OLD TOWN When Kasper Pollera first opened this hotel, Napoleon had not long been buried. Enjoying its grand period a century ago before being occupied by the Nazis, then left to decay, the hardy Pollera has been handed back to its rightful owners and brought back into service. Guests are treated to comfortable if not luxurious lodgings, but most are happy to pass by the wonderful original stained-glass artwork by Stanisław Wyspiański on the staircase while contemplating 180 years of history. *Ul.Szpitalna 30.* ☎ *012/422-10-44. www.pollera. com.pl. 42 units. Doubles 300 zł. AE, DC, MC, V. All trams to Old Town. Map p 133.*

Polonia NEAR OLD TOWN Opened opposite the train station in 1917, the Polonia is one of several hotels in town gradually shedding decades of post-war neglect. The rooms are a mixed bag of modernized and vintage, though none are tatty and the location on the edge of the Old Town can't be beat. *Ul.Basztowa 25.* ☎ *012/ 422-12-33. www.hotel-polonia.com.pl. 61 units. Doubles 240 zł–300 zł. AE, DC, MC, V. All trams to Dworzec Główny. Map p 133.*

★★★ **Pugetów** NEAR OLD TOWN The jewel in the Donimirski crown, the outstanding Pugetów was opened in 2003, in one of a cluster of 19th-century buildings set in from the main road linking the Old Town to Kazimierz. Rooms have been individually furnished in historic style according to character name—Napoleon's Polish lover Pani Walewska or Joseph Conrad, for example. The result encourages repeat custom all year round. This is honeymoon material, so relax and enjoy one of the most impressive lodgings in all Poland. *Ul.Starowiślna 15a.* ☎ *012/432-49-50. www.donimirski.com. 7 units. Doubles 380 zł–470 zł. All trams to Starowiślna. AE, DC, MC, V. Map p 133.*

★★★ **Qubus Hotel** PODGÓRZE The Qubus goes about things in a suitably businesslike fashion, providing a first-class breakfast in the Ogień restaurant, decent cocktails in the Barracuda lobby bar, and entertainment in the Mile Stone jazz club (p 127) and After Work bar. It also has the best pool area in the city, if only for the rooftop panorama as you swim your lengths, laze in the Jacuzzi, or stretch out on a recliner. *Ul.Nadwiślańska 6.* ☎ *012/ 374-51-00. www.qubushotel.com. 194 units. Doubles 575 zł. AE, DC, MC, V. All trams to Pl.Bohaterów Getta. Map p 134.*

★ **Radisson Blu** NEAR OLD TOWN You know what you're getting with a

The Stary is a converted 15th-century merchant's house.

Radisson. This one is located prominently on the edge of the Planty ring just outside the Old Town. The reliable service and quality of fare is as to be expected in the Milk&Co and Salt&Co bar and restaurant. Individuality has been added with local artwork in each of the 196 rooms. *Ul.Straszewskiego 17.* ☎ *012/618-88-88. www.radissonblu.com. 196 units. Doubles 565 zł–774 zł. AE, DC, MC, V. All trams to Filharmonia. Map p 133.*

Rezydent OLD TOWN   Reopened in March 2011 after a partial renovation, this pleasant three-star is conveniently situated close to the main market square. Standard rooms all now have Wi-Fi, but can still only be accessed by the stairs. Superior rooms are now kitted out with new furniture, and all units have been tastefully decorated. Little wrong either with the restaurant, the Pod Gwiazdami, where hotel guests receive a handy discount. *Ul.Grodzka 9.* ☎ *012/429-54-10. www.rezydent. krakow.pl. 59 units. Doubles 375 zł–455 zł. AE, DC, MC, V. All trams to Old Town. Map p 133.*

★★ **Rubinstein** KAZIMIERZ   Italian marble in the bathrooms, carpets of New Zealand wool in the bedrooms, and neo-Renaissance touches throughout, this is the most stylish place to stay in Kazimierz. Room rates reflect the high standard but in the quieter summer weeks you should be able to find a bargain online. No beating the location either, the whole of the Jewish quarter spread out before you from the roof terrace. The quality bar and restaurant complete the picture. *Ul.Szeroka 12.* ☎ *012/384-00-00. www.hotel rubinstein.com. 27 units. Doubles 480 zł–700 zł. AE, DC, MC, V. Tram 7, 9, 11, 13, 24: Miodowa. Map p 133.*

★★ **Senacki** OLD TOWN   A conversion of a historic building on the Royal Route, the Senacki comprises 20 finely decorated rooms, including two luxury ones, a penthouse, and the cheaper attic. The lack of a lift keeps the Senacki at three-star status—but the frequently returning visitors know class when they see it. The restaurant receives healthy custom from non-residents. *Ul.Grodzka 51.* ☎ *012/422-76-86. www.hotel senacki.pl. 20 units. Doubles 450 zł–540 zł. AE, DC, MC, V. All trams to Old Town. Map p 133.*

★★ **Sheraton Krakow** NEAR WAWEL   Set by the Vistula just under Wawel, the Sheraton accommodates guests to its usual high standards. High-speed Internet in the comfortable rooms, separate saunas for men and women, a heated indoor pool, and a range of massage treatments are key here, while non-residents are brought in by the 200-odd vodkas available in the QUBE bar, the Tex-Mex food and TV sports at SomePlace Else bar, and the Med cuisine on offer at The Olive. *Ul.Powiśle 7.* ☎ *012/662-10-00. www.sheraton. pl/krakow. 232 units. Doubles 535 zł–1,025 zł. AE, DC, MC, V. All trams to Jubilat. Map p 134.*

★★★ **Stary** OLD TOWN   Quite possibly the best hotel in Krakow,

The 16th-century Tango House, originally Krakow's first bathhouse.

the Stary is a converted merchant's house, originally built in the 15th century. The Likus group has really gone to town—a glass lift, marble, silk, exotic woods, and Oriental carpets, two heated pools (one with massage jets), a salt cave, Finnish and steam saunas, and yoga among the many treatments. Even the single rooms have Jacuzzi tubs. In summer they open a rooftop terrace with bar—in colder months, the quality Trzy Rybki restaurant more than compensates. *Ul.Szczepańska 5.* ☎ *012/384-08-08. www.hotel stary.com. 53 units. Doubles 690 zł–900 zł. AE, DC, MC, V. All trams to Old Town. Map p 133.*

★ **Tango House** OLD TOWN So close to the main market square you can hear the bugler, this is one of the city's best bed and breakfasts. Converted in 2007 from a 16th-century property—Krakow's first public bathhouse, in fact—the Tango House is decked out in bright colors and contemporary furnishings. Ambient tango music can be switched on with the push of a dial. A decent cold buffet is laid out for breakfast and a laptop is provided for guests' use in the cafe. *Ul.Szpitalna 4.* ☎ *012/429-31-14. www.tango house.pl. 8 units. Doubles 199 zł–340 zł. AE, DC, MC, V. All trams to Old Town. Map p 133.*

★ **Trecius** OLD TOWN Named after the secretary to István Batory acknowledged to have lived here in the 16th century, this town house was probably built 300 years earlier. It's one of Krakow's best located and most characterful guesthouses—you can even make out some of the 13th-century brickwork amid the exposed stones. Rooms have been kitted out with contemporary touches—satellite TV, Internet, and heated bathroom floors—and a flick through the visitors' book should assure you of the hotel's conviviality. *Ul.Św.Tomasza 18.* ☎ *012/421-25-21. www.trecius.krakow.pl. 8 units. Doubles 150 zł–300 zł. AE, DC, MC, V. All trams to Old Town. Map p 133.*

★ **Unicus** OLD TOWN A well-appointed newbie in the Old Town, the Unicus is also convenient for business travelers using the station

The sumptuous Wentzl.

The Wyspiański, near Old Town.

or train service to the airport. There are conference facilities, a gym, sauna, and top-class restaurant in a beautiful old building where Floriańska meets Św.Marka. The management has also had the foresight to hire Poland's leading chef, Rafał Targosz, to thrust the hotel into the spotlight with his contemporary takes on Polish cuisine in the restaurant. *Ul.Floriańska 35.* ☎ *012/433-71-11. www.hotelunicus.pl. 35 units. Doubles 500 zł–700 zł. AE, DC, MC, V. All trams to Old Town. Map p 133.*

★ **Wawel** OLD TOWN In private hands for nearly 2 decades, this former 19th-century inn has undergone many improvements and today ranks as one of the best midrange deals in Krakow. Guest rooms are spacious and homely, in calming colors and equipped with flatscreen TVs. The Jacuzzi and steam rooms are paid extras. *Ul.Poselska 22.* ☎ *012/424-13-00. www.hotelwawel. pl. 39 units. Doubles 350 zł–460 zł. AE, DC, MC, V. All trams to Old Town. Map p 133.*

★★★ **Wentzl** OLD TOWN Rightfully considered one of the finest lodgings in all Poland, this sumptuous 200-year-old landmark comprises 18 opulent guest rooms, many overlooking the main square. Dark woods, richly colored rugs, and parquet floors feature throughout. The staff are used to dealing with dignitaries and important guests, and will happily book your theater ticket or city tour. The inhouse terrace restaurant is a destination in itself. *Rynek Główny 19.* ☎ *012/430-26-64. www.wentzl.pl. 18 units. Doubles 510 zł–630 zł. AE, DC, MC, V. All trams to Old Town. Map p 133.*

Wyspiański NEAR OLD TOWN Built in the 1960s, this behemoth on the Planty ring was completely renovated in 2003 and now operates as an attractive three-star conference hotel. Busloads of tourists pull up in the wide forecourt all year round—individual travelers should look out for online deals and all-in packages set around special events in town. *Ul.Westerplatte 15.* ☎ *012/422-95-66. www.hotel-wyspianski.pl. 158 units. Doubles 195 zł–440 zł. AE, DC, MC, V. All trams to Poczta Główna. Map p 133.* ●

10 The Best Day Trips & Excursions

Auschwitz

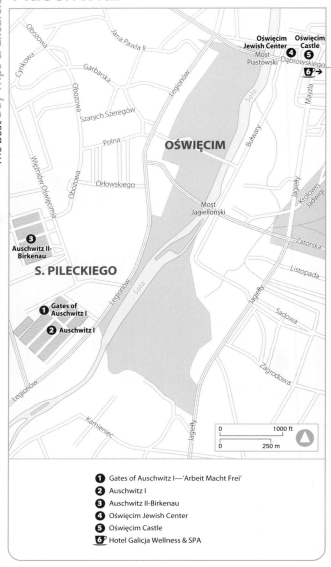

① Gates of Auschwitz I—'Arbeit Macht Frei'

② Auschwitz I

③ Auschwitz II-Birkenau

④ Oświęcim Jewish Center

⑤ Oświęcim Castle

⑥ Hotel Galicja Wellness & SPA

Previous page: The beautiful Polish countryside.

Preserved as a museum in 1947 as it was found, Auschwitz attracts busloads of tourists, many from Krakow. For independent visits, a guide is essential, but not obligatory. Two camps sit 3km (1.9 miles) apart: Auschwitz I, its huts and one surviving gas chamber; and vast Auschwitz II–Birkenau, whose guard tower, gate, and rails remain. Auschwitz (Oświęcim) town is nearby.

❶ ★★ **Gates of Auschwitz I— 'Arbeit Macht Frei'.** Nearly everyone standing at these gates has seen them in film or photo form—to stand here, before the hour-long tour of the first and best-preserved camp, is a chilling feeling. The motto, "Work Makes You Free," was used at other camps. Here, bizarrely, it is used in a 1920s' typeface with an upside-down "B" in "Arbeit." What you see here today is a replica—the original sign was stolen in 2009, cut up and recovered shortly afterwards. Just inside the gates are drawings by Miecław Kościelniak (1912–93), Auschwitz survivor, founder of the museum, and an artist of global renown. An orchestra would play at the beginning of the working day—and at the end, inmates carrying the corpses of their exhausted colleagues. ⏱ *10 min.*

❷ ★★★ **Auschwitz I.** Concentration camps in the Nazi Reich were used for either slave labor or immediate execution. Auschwitz was both a work camp and a death camp. It comprises neat rows of 28 huts, half converted for public display, either by theme ("Everyday Life of the Prisoner," "Extermination") or provenance (Poland, Yugoslavia, European Roma). Tours also take in Death Block 11; Assembly Square with a reconstruction of its portable gallows; and the one remaining gas chamber of the original four. You may have to wait outside one block as tour groups file out. Of particular resonance are the suitcases, piles of human hair, and children's shoes, as found by Soviet soldiers in 1945; the starvation cells of block 11, in particular number 18 where Polish priest Maximilian Kolbe sacrificed his life for a fellow prisoner; and the adjoining Wall of Death, against which thousands of prisoners were shot, today strewn with flowers and flags in the colors of the Auschwitz

The gates of Auschwitz I.

Practical Matters: Auschwitz

Auschwitz (Polish name on maps, signs, and timetables: Oświęcim) is 75km (47 miles) from Krakow. Nearly all tour companies offer guided visits to Auschwitz, for about 90 zł. Allow half a day. Regular city buses leave from Ul.Bosacka behind the train station, for Oświęcim train and bus stations, 90 minutes journey time. Some call at Auschwitz I. A less frequent train service takes the same time and costs around the same, less than 15 zł. A dozen local buses link Oświęcim station with Auschwitz I. Oświęcim town center is on the east bank of the river from the train station. Those on guided tours from Krakow are bussed the 3km (1.9 miles) from Auschwitz I to Birkenau; for independent visitors, an hourly shuttle bus runs from mid-April to November. A taxi should cost about 15 zł.

prisoners' uniforms, blue and white. Nothing, though, can match the feeling of walking into the bare gas chamber, cramped, claustrophobic, a track on its floor leading a few meters to the ovens alongside. This is the last stop on any tour. There is a cafe and shop by the museum entrance, and more amenities across the parking lot. ⏱ *1 hr. Ul.Więzniów Oświęcim 20.* ☎ *033/ 844-80-00. www.auschwitz.org.pl. Admission Nov–Mar free; individual guided tours (English language) 40 zł; groups vary. Apr–Oct groups only. Daily June–Aug 8am–7pm; May, Sept 8am–6pm; Apr, Oct 8am– 5pm; Mar, Nov 8am–4pm; Dec–Feb 8am–3pm. Children under 12 advised not to enter. All buses, trains, and minibuses to Oświęcim. Frequent guided tours from Krakow.*

❸ ★★★ **Auschwitz II–Birkenau.** Birkenau was built to cope with the huge influx of European Jewry, particularly from Hungary. It was little but a death factory—you can see the rails leading from the gates to the crematorium. Climb the

Auschwitz II-Birkenau.

stairs to the watchtower over the gates and there are brick stumps as far as the eye can see, remnants of the barracks that held prisoners in conditions barely fit for cattle. Your guide will point out the gaps between roof and thin wall of the example hut—there was little difference between the temperature outside and in. At full capacity, the ovens consumed 60,000 victims a day. On the camp's northern fringe is a pond still gray from the human ashes dumped there. Birkenau is bare, lacking in visitor amenities but worth seeing, if only to appreciate the scale of what transpired. ⏲ *40 min. Same details as above.*

❹ ★★ **Oświęcim Jewish Center.** Opened in 2000, the year that the last Jewish resident of Oświęcim, Szymon Kluger (1925–2000), died, and set beside the town's only surviving synagogue, this laudable institution is dedicated to keeping local Jewish culture alive. A video of interviews with surviving residents is shown in English, the main attraction of the museum also filled with photographs, documents, and sundry artifacts relating to pre-war life in Oświęcim, whose local population of 15,000 in 1939 was half Jewish. Soon after, the Nazis converted the synagogue into a munitions warehouse, and the Communists turned it into a carpet warehouse—it was returned to the Jewish community and restored for 2000. Although services are no longer given, this is considered a place of sanctuary. A nearby Education Center hosts seminars, talks, and cultural events. Opposite the museum, you can visit Kluger's house as he left it in 2000. ⏲ *45 min. Pl.ks.Jana Skarbka 3–5.* ☎ *033/844-70-02. www.ajcf.pl. Train or bus to Oświęcim.*

❺ ★ **Oświęcim Castle.** Set between the Jewish Center and Synagogue and the Sola river it overlooks, Oświęcim Castle demonstrates the generations of citizens who lived here. Its 13th-century Gothic tower, currently being renovated, was built after the Tartar invasion, and other elements were added after further invasion, fire, and flood: Defensive walls, a moat, armory, and living quarters. A modest historical exhibition awaits expansion once current renovations are complete. Tours from Krakow do not go into Oświęcim town—you are generally welcome to ask the guide to drop you off at the station—a short walk over the river from town—and make your own way back. ⏲ *30 min. Ul.Zamkowa 1.* ☎ *033/842-44-27. http://museum-zamek.pl. Admission 3 zł adults, 2 zł children. July, Aug Tues, Thurs 10am–4pm, Wed 10am–6pm, Fri 10am–3pm, Sat, Sun 11am–3pm; May, June, Sept Mon, Tues, Thurs 10am–4pm; Wed 10am–6pm, Fri 10am–3pm, Sun 11am–3pm; Oct–Apr Mon–Thurs 10am–4pm, Fri 10am–3pm, Sun 11am–3pm. Train or bus to Oświęcim.*

❻ ★ **Hotel Galicja Wellness & SPA.** The best hotel in town, a renovated old post house, provides the best spots to eat and drink in Oświęcim town: The U Szwejka cellar pub with original 19th-century brick walls; and the first-floor Stara Poczta restaurant, serving traditional Polish and Silesian favorites. It's far nearer to the bus station than to the train, so if you're returning to Krakow under your own steam, and ending your visit here (there are 32 rooms too), bus is the best way back. *Ul.Dąbrowskiego 119, Oświęcim.* ☎ *030/843-61-15. www.hotelgalicja.com. zł zł.*

Ojców

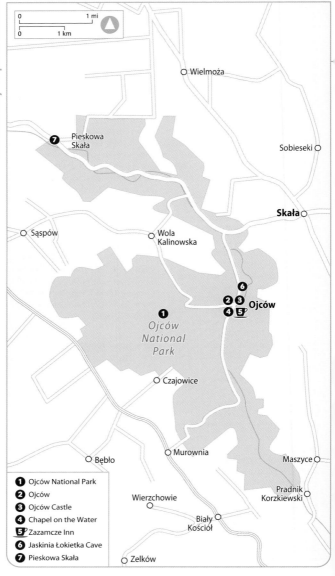

0		1 mi
0	1 km	

O Wielmoża

Pieskowa
Skała ⑦

Sobieseki O

Skała O

O Sąspów

O Wola
Kalinowska

⑥
② ③ Ojców
④ ⑤

①
*Ojców
National
Park*

O Czajowice

O Bębło

O Murownia

Maszyce O

Wierzchowie
O

Pradnik
Korzkiewski

Biały O
Kościół

O Zelków

① Ojców National Park
② Ojców
③ Ojców Castle
④ Chapel on the Water
⑤ Zazamcze Inn
⑥ Jaskinia Łokietka Cave
⑦ Pieskowa Skała

Ojców, Krakow's closest national park, is associated with rocks and royals. In the river valley of the Prądnik, its caves hid King Władisłw Łokietek from the Bohemians. His son, Kazimierz the Great, built 25 castles, the Eagle Nests Trail. Many travel the 35km (22 miles) from Krakow for the birds and the butterflies that call the unspoiled hills home.

❶ ★★★ Ojców National Park.

Poland's smallest national park, a short and easy hop north from Krakow, comprises the limestone valley of the Prądnik river, the hundreds of caves and weird rock formations it has created, and the abundance of wildlife and plant varieties engendered by its microclimate. It is also the southern fringe of the **Eagle Nests Trail,** a 165-km (102-mile) long string of 25 medieval strongholds commissioned by Kazimierz the Great, now a popular route for hikers and cyclists. A ruined one stands outside the village of Ojców, administrative base for the surrounding park. One of the most stunning is **Pieskowa Skała,** built in Renaissance style at the northern border of the national park. ⏱ *2 hr. 32-047 Ojców.* ☎ *012/389-20-05.*

www.ojcow.pl. Free admission. Guided day tours in English 450 zł. Bus or train from Krakow to Ojców.

❷ ★★ Ojców.

Set in the center of the park, the pretty village of Ojców sits in the **Prądnik valley,** a community of 220 souls living in wooden chalets set against a fabulous backdrop of woods and cliffs. It's a treat in fall or winter—and filled with hikers, bikers, and parties of schoolchildren all year round. For all its natural beauty, this modest settlement has a surprising number of manmade attractions. By the bus terminus, Władysław Szafer's **Natural History Museum** (closed Mon, also Sat, Sun in winter) contains remains of mammoths and other prehistoric creatures; nearby are the tourist office and a **Regional Museum** lined with folk costumes and old prints of the

Ojców National Park.

Practical Matters: Ojców

Ojców village is 35km (21.7 miles) north of Krakow. Two buses a day leave from Krakow bus station, behind the train station, for Olkusz, calling at Ojców after an hour. Eight buses a day go to Ojców Park, two fast ones early in the morning taking around 40 minutes. By car, head north past Ikea and Macro until you hit the roundabout turn for Olkusz, keeping on road 94. Ojców is soon signposted. Bicycles can follow this same route, but a nicer one is along the **Eagle Nests Trail,** heading from Krowodrza along side roads—you'll find a map on **www.ojcow.pl**. There's also a fast bike route via road 794—again, check the website.

village. The main draws are the ruined Ojców Castle and the nearby Chapel on the Water, attracting thousands to Ojców every summer. ⏱ *1 hr. Tourist office Ojców 15.* ☎ *012/ 389-20-10. www.ojcow.pttk.pl. Bus or train from Krakow to Ojców.*

❸ ★ **Ojców Castle.** The southernmost of the string of strongholds built by Kazimierz the Great, Ojców is a Gothic ruin, its original towers still erect and circled by bats. Also standing are the gatehouse and walls of the keep—the moat and

Gate house, Ojców Castle.

well have long since been filled in. Although most of the walls collapsed in the 1820s, the castle is still worth a visit for the gloomy, historic atmosphere and the view of the woods and the valley. ⏱ *30 min.* ☎ *012/389-20-44. Admission 2.50 zł adults, 1.50 zł children. Apr–May, Aug–Sept Tues–Sun 10am–4:45pm; June–July Tues–Sun 10am–5:45pm; Oct Tues–Sun 10am–3:45pm.*

❹ ★★ **Chapel on the Water.** This anomaly was opened in 1901, a rustic chapel perched over the Prądnik river as the then ruling Tsar Nikolai II had forbidden the building of any places of worship in regional territory—on land at least. The building is in the shape of a cross, conforming to so-called Ojców style. You can take a peek at the interior in between services on Sundays. ⏱ *20 min.*

❺ ★ **Zazamcze Inn.** Easily the best dining option around these parts is this pretty chalet surrounded by greenery, known for its grilled trout and barbecued pork. This is quality fare in a quality setting—hence the wedding parties and tourist groups. There are a dozen rooms too, should you

Pieskowa Skała.

choose to stay over. You'll find it just outside Ojców village. *32-047 Ojców 1B.* ☎ *012/389-20-83. www.zajazd zazamcze.ojcow.pl. zł.*

❻ ★ Jaskinia Łokietka Cave. Some 2.5km (1.5 miles) from Ojców village, a 45-minute walk, this is the largest and most famous of the hundreds of caves dotted around the national park. Named after the so-called King "Shorty" (Łokietek), Kazimierz's father, who allegedly hid here from the Bohemian Vaclav II, this illuminated cave is some 250m (820 ft.) long. Visits are guided only and last about 30 minutes—take warm clothes as the temperature is less than 10°C (50°F). There are said to be seven breeds of bats, resident here for centuries. ⏱ *20 min.* ☎ *012/ 423-90-63. Admission 7 zł adults, 5 zł children. Daily spring, fall 9am–3:30pm (latest 4:30pm), summer 9am–6:30pm.*

❼ ★★★ Pieskowa Skała. The jewel in Ojców's crown, and a rare perfectly preserved castle in the Eagle Nests Trail, stands 9km (5.6 miles) from Ojców village, an easy 45-minute walk away. On your way you'll pass the limestone pillar known as **Hercules' Club**—the castle is just behind. Once a stronghold in the medieval fashion, under the aristocratic Szafraniec family, it gained an arcaded Renaissance courtyard. Equally attractive to the thousands of annual tourists is the exhibition of European art contained here, part of the Wawel collection, featuring baroque rooms lined with fine Flemish tapestries showing the life of Alexander the Great, and Gothic carvings from the 1400s. An extension of the exhibit will cover the period from the 18th century to the early 20th once it is completed. A stroll around the fine gardens should round off your visit nicely. ⏱ *40 min. Ul.Sułoszowa 4.* ☎ *012/389-60-04. www.pieskowaskala.pl. Admission 10 zł adults, 7 zł children. Summer Tues–Thurs 9am–5pm, Fri 9am–1pm, Sat, Sun 10am–6pm; Apr, Sept Tues–Thurs 10am–4pm, Fri 10am–1pm, Sat, Sun 10am–4pm; Nov–Mar Tues–Fri groups only, Sat, Sun 10am–4pm.*

Zakopane

0		1.5 mi
0	1.5 km	

Ząb

Poronin

Gliczarów Górny

Tatrzańska

Jana Kasprowicza

Droga Do Olczy

Sądelska

Murzasichle

Małe Ciche

Area of Zakopane inset

Kościeliska

Zakopane

Strazyska

Tatrzański Park Narodowy

POLSKA

SLOVENSKÁ REPUBLIKA

1 Zakopane
2 Karcma Po Zboju
3 Tatra Museum
4 Zakopane Style Museum
5 Władysław Hasior Gallery
6 Karcma Zapiecek
7 Gubalówka Hill
8 Kasprowy Wierch
9 Morskie Oko
10 Café Piano

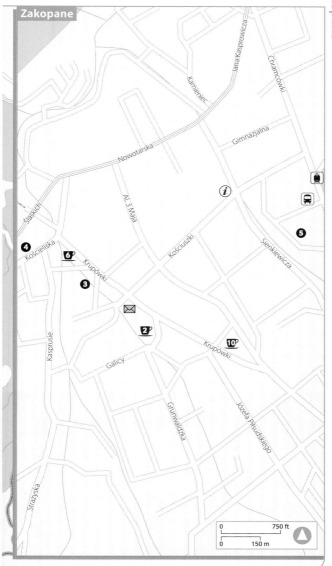

The highest town in Poland, down south by the Slovak border, Zakopane is where Poles go to ski, hike, and hang out for the weekend—often, it feels, on the very same weekend. Expect lines and traffic jams on major winter breaks. The gateway to the Tatra mountains, Zakopane allows access to the funicular to Gubalówka Hill and glacial lake of Morskie Oko.

❶ ★★★ kids Zakopane. With regular buses, trains only a few hours from Krakow, and roads jam-packed for winter weekends, Zakopane is southern Poland's favorite getaway. Its skiing facilities so plentiful it was a reasonable candidate for a recent Winter Olympics, Zakopane has a century of experience in accommodating tourists. First the fresh air began attracting hikers and health tourists here on doctor's advice in the 1870s; then a bohemian atmosphere arose when writers and artists from the Młoda Polska movement used Zakopane as a place to create, make merry, and foment revolution. Today the town center, and its main street of **Krupówki,** still display both the chalet charm of those days and the commercial clout of a major tourist destination. Within walking distance of the bus and train stations to the east of the Krupówki hub are a handful of worthwhile regional museums and galleries, and a funicular to **Gubalówka Hill,** the closest and busiest summit. A 20-minute walk south of town, regularly served by local buses, is the small village of **Kuźnice,** site of the busy cable car to **Kasprowy Wierch,** the highest of the near-2,000-m (6,560-ft.) peaks forming the border with Slovakia. *Tourist information Ul.Kościuszki 17.* ☎ *018/201-22-11. www.zakopane. pl. All buses and trains to Zakopane.*

❷ ★ kids Karcma Po Zboju. On the main drag, this bar-restaurant in traditional style offers local specialties from breakfast (white sausage, the famed local cheeses) onwards. Cakes, pies, and puddings are another strong point. A garden in equally rustic style contains a seesaw, slide, and treehouse. An ideal

Traditional house in Zakopane.

Trekking in the Tatra mountains.

first port of call to freshen up after your arrival, find your bearings, and get acquainted with the locality. *Ul.Krupówki 22b.* ☎ *018/201-61-40. http://karczmapozboju.pl. zlzl.*

❸ ★★ Tatra Museum. The distinguished Tatra Museum is formed of several divisions, including the Zakopane Style Museum and Hasior Gallery, with information for each found on the same website. This main branch is of historical interest in itself—the building was designed by Stanisław Witkiewicz (1885–1939), an influential painter, playwright, and architect of the pre-war Zakopane circle. Inside, two floors display the history of the region through the ages, from prehistoric traces to Zakopane's heyday in the late 1800s. The rapid rise of tourism and culture are covered hand-in-hand—the development of sanatoria and skiing, as well as a theater company and a local press. A replica of a typical cottage, plus examples of ceramics, tools, and traditional costumes, show the way of life that attracted so many here from Krakow in the early 20th century—Zakopane was where Poles could express their patriotism openly. The top floor deals with natural history, showing the geology of the mountain range, examples of local plants and stuffed animals, the protected Tatra chamois goat, and so on. All in all, the museum provides a detailed

Practical Matters: Zakopane

Zakopane town is served by buses every hour from Krakow (regular journey time around 2½ hours, tickets about 15 zł). Traffic jams on busy winter weekends are frequent—allow 3 hours. The drive via roads 7 and 47 should be 90 minutes. If you're thinking of hiring a car, Zakopane has a decent supply of parking places, but the town itself is easily walkable and bus services to nearby attractions are cheap and regular. Private rooms, pensions, hostels, and hotels are equally plentiful, but book ahead in high season, summer or winter.

and entertaining stroll through local history. ⏱ *1 hr. Ul.Krupówki 10.* ☎ *018/201-52-05. www.muzeum tatrzanskie.com.pl. Admission 7 zł adults, 5.50 zł children. May 10–Sept 30 Tues–Sat 9am–5pm, Sun 9am–3pm; Oct 1–May 9 Wed Sat 9am–5pm, Sun 9am–3pm.*

❹ ★★ Zakopane Style Museum.

Another Witkiewicz building, the Koliba Willa, is an apt setting for an illustration of the architectural vernacular of Zakopane, a modern revision of traditional methods instigated by Witkiewicz himself at the turn of the past century. Many pieces were collated by estate owner Zygmunt Gnatowski, a friend of Witkiewicz, and bequeathed to the artist. The house itself went through several changes, including occupation by the Nazis, before this collection of ethnic fittings and furniture was set out by contemporary installation artist Władysław Hasior (1928–99) and opened as a museum in the early 1990s. It comprises seven rooms, filled with ornate but sturdy chairs and cupboards, tools, folksy tiles, and curtains. ⏱ *30 min. Koliba Willa,*

Ul.Kościeliska 18. ☎ *018/201-36-02. www.muzeumtatrzaskie.com.pl. Admission 7 zł adults, 5.50 zł children. Wed–Sat 9am–5pm, Sun 9am–3pm.*

❺ ★★ Władysław Hasior Gallery.

The best-known Zakopane artist of the 20th century, Władysław Hasior displayed many regional influences in his paintings and installations, exhibited across Europe in the 1960s and 1970s. Banners, sculptures, and paintings exude bright colors and essentially Polish themes, albeit with a great deal of wit and irreverence—this was art with little censorship, as ever was in Zakopane. The gallery was opened in the mid-1980s, a decade before the artist's death. ⏱ *30 min. Ul.Koziniec 8.* ☎ *018/206-68-71. www.muzeumtatrzaskie.com.pl. Admission 7 zł adults, 5.50 zł children. Wed–Sat 11am–6pm, Sun 9am–3pm.*

❻ ★ Karcma Zapiecek.

This rustic restaurant on the main street is the ideal spot for a lunchtime stop-off to load up on carbohydrates and

Kasprowy Ski Resort.

Mount Kasprowy Wierch.

regional dishes made with local sheep's milk cheeses before you attack the slopes. If you're heading here in the evening for an après-ski fill-up, you might be entertained with a little live folk music. *Ul.Krupówki 43.* ☎ *018/201-56-99. http://zapiecek.pl. zlzl.*

❼ ★★★ kids Gubalówka Hill.

This nursery ski run is the perfect introduction to the Tatra slopes, easily accessed by funicular a short walk from downtown Zakopane— simply stroll to the far western end of Krupówki and join the line. At the top you'll find the terrace restaurant **Gubalówka** (☎ **018/206-36-30**), stores selling sundry souvenirs, and far too many hamburger stands for comfort. You can't beat the views of the surrounding slopes, though, and kids will enjoy the pony rides, mini-bobsled, and pay telescopes. Several hiking trails also start from here, or you can walk back down—a great deal easier than the calf-crunching, hour-long climb uphill. ⏱ *2 hr.* ☎ *018/201-48-30. Funicular return*

20 zł. *Daily July–Aug 7am–9pm. Sept–June 8am–5pm.*

❽ ★★★ Kasprowy Wierch. For

the real Tatra experience, jump on one of the many buses covering the 3-km (1.9-mile) journey from Zakopane to Kuźnice to ride the cable car to the 2,000m (6,560-ft.) summit of Kasprowy Wierch. The mountain forms the Polish–Slovak border— you can walk over into another country. Because of the lines in high season, many choose to walk up or down the mountain, a trek of around 2 to 3 hours. At the top there are scientific observatories, opened around the same time as the cable car was installed in the 1930s, and a panoramic restaurant. A return ticket on the cable car allows you 2 hours at the top. A number of firms offer skiing lessons from intermediate upwards, and advance tickets on the cable car. ⏱ *2 hr. www.discoverzakopane. com. Cable car return 40 zł. Daily July–Aug 7:30am–8pm. Sept–June 8am–5pm.*

Morskie Oko.

Hard Cheese

Wherever you go in Zakopane, you're bound to see an old lady selling little bundles of **oscypek**—local cheese made from heavily salted unpasteurized sheep's milk. Each takes at least 2 weeks to produce, the bundle shaped into a pretty pattern, soaked in a barrel full of brine, and then placed for 10 days or more under the roof of a typical wooden house to be smoked slowly and thus gain its distinctive flavor. This is how *oscypek* has been made in the Tatras for generations. Shortly before Poland joined the E.U. in 2004, there was an outcry that bureaucrats in Brussels might ban Zakopane's signature cheese due to its use of unpasteurized milk. Locals feared that their whole way of life would vanish—protests were prepared and politicians badgered. In the end, the humble *oscypek* received the status of E.U. Protected Designation of Origin, much like Camembert or Champagne. Providing it comes from Tatras, and it is produced in this way, *oscypek* is *oscypek*, Zakopane's favorite salty snack.

⑨ ★★★ Morskie Oko. This gorgeous glacial lake is one of Zakopane's big draws—many a restaurant in Poland serving regional highlander cuisine is named after it. The starting point for the 2-hour hike to reach it is a large parking lot at **Polana Palenica** (also called Polana Białczanska), connected by regular bus or minibus from Zakopane or nearby Łysa Polana. There a gaggle of hikers of all types and ages gather, before paying a couple of złotys to enter the national park and the tarmac trail leading up through the trees. Local highlanders still work horse-drawn sleighs and carriages according to season from here to 1.5km (or just under a mile) before the summit for those not keen on the walk—price negotiable. Surrounded by towering peaks, the "Eye of the Sea" makes any climb worthwhile—it's a stunning sight.

The **Schronisko przy Morskim Oku** mountain hut (www.schronisko morskieoko.pl) stands at the northern edge, offering bunk beds for climbers and basic domestic meals. Expect it to take around an hour to walk around the lake. ⏱ *4 hr.*

⑩ ★ Café Piano. Pull up a velvet-seated swing at the bar counter and help yourself to a well-earned beer or cocktail at the trendiest bar in Zakopane, in a little alley just off the main street. The Piano manages to combine rustic and contemporary—note the amber and touches of greenery. It's a little cramped so can get packed on busy winter weekends but that's a minor gripe. It's a good place too for picking up flyers and brochures for what's on in town. *Ul.Krupówki 63.* ☎ *018/201-21-08. zł.* ●

The
Savvy Traveler

Before You Go

Government Tourist Offices

Poland National Tourist Office (PNTO): In the U.S. & Canada: 5 Marine View Plaza, Suite 303b, Hoboken, New Jersey, NJ 07030-5722 (☎ **201/420-9910;** www.poland.travel/en-us). **In the U.K.:** Westgate House, West Gate, London W5 1YY (☎ **0300/303-1814;** www.poland-travel/en-gb).

The Best Times to Go

With a steady influx of low-fare airline passengers, Krakow is Poland's most popular destination, attracting tourists **all year round.** The busiest time is in the **summer,** when the city fills with busloads of tour groups and backpackers. Sudden hot spells can occur but the weather is put to good use with a handful of outdoor cultural events and festivals. **Spring and fall** are more favorable but be prepared for rain showers. The changing colors of the Planty greenery are a thing to behold in September. **Winters** can be bitterly cold and dark—but the run-up to **Christmas** is wonderfully atmospheric, market stalls and cribs set around the main market square. Poles flood into Krakow for **All Saints' Day,** November 1, and visit the city's cemeteries. Krakow is used as a base to visit the hiking and skiing region of Zakopane (p 158) by Poles, Slovaks, and other foreigners for winter weekends.

Hotel prices drop in the quieter times of year, on weekdays after New Year until March and during November and early December. Prices rise at Easter, for New Year, and in the height of summer.

Festivals & Special Events

SPRING. Easter (Wielkanoc) is the most important religious festival of the year. Locals enjoy jam doughnuts and sweet pastries before Lent and observe a period of fasting or lean meals in the run-up to **Good Friday.** On **Palm Sunday,** palm processions take place across the city and churches fill for mass on **Easter Sunday.** On **Easter Monday** before noon, the menfolk splash women with water or cheap perfume, a fertility ritual that may stretch to people chucking buckets of water out of windows.

In **April,** as part of the **Days of Organ Music Festival** (www.filharmonia.krakow.pl), concerts are given in churches across Krakow.

Two public holidays in early May see locals take trips and breaks out of town: **Labor Day** on May 1, and **Constitution Day** on May 3, when a wreath is laid at the Tomb of the Unknown Soldier on Plac Matejki. The **Krakow Film Festival** (www.kff.com) takes place later in the month.

SUMMER. A variety of events and concerts under the umbrella of the **City of Krakow Festival** (www.krakow.pl) is held in squares and public spaces across the city. Locals gather by the riverbank for fireworks on Midsummer's Eve, the **Feast of St. John.** From late June until early July, for the **Festival of Jewish Culture** (www.jewishfestival.pl) concerts, readings, and exhibitions are staged in major venues around Kazimierz. In early July, **Ulica 24 Street Art** (http://teatrkto.pl) offers

AVERAGE TEMPERATURE & RAINFALL IN KRAKOW

	JAN	FEB	MAR	APR	MAY	JUNE
Daily Temp. (°C)	-4	-2	3	9	14	17
Daily Temp. (°F)	25	28	37	48	57	62
Rainfall (mm/in.)	38/1.5	27/1.06	26/1.02	30/1.18	30/1.18	3/1.7

	JULY	AUG	SEPT	OCT	NOV	DEC
Daily Temp. (°C)	18	18	14	5	4	-1
Daily Temp. (°F)	64	64	57	41	39	30
Rainfall (mm/in.)	71/2.8	66/2.6	66/2.6	48/1.9	53/2.08	40/1.57

free international street theater in the main square. Also in July, the **Krakow Jazz Festival** (www.crac jazz.com) is held in prominent music bars and cellars in the Old Town.

In August, the main market square and adjoining Maly Rynek accommodate a weekend of food tasting and concerts: The annual **Pierogi Festival** (www.biuro festiwalowe.pl). August 15, the **Feast of the Assumption,** is a national public holiday. The 2-day **Coke Live Festival** (http://live festival.pl) in mid-August has been staged since 2006, featuring big-name artists from the world of pop, R&B, and hip-hop. Previous guests have included Kanye West, Lily Allen, and the Chemical Brothers. The current venue is the Aviation Museum (p 35). Around the same time, over the last 2 weeks in August, **Music in Old Krakow** (www.capellacroviensis.pl) features Polish music through the ages at historic venues.

FALL. The biggest event in the local music calendar, **Sacrum Profanum** (www.sacrumprofanum.com/en), calls for performers of major international standing to give shows in industrial and ex-industrial settings across the city. Each year is themed after a certain nation or region. Concerts are held over a few days in mid-September. For **All Saints' Day,** November 1, a public holiday,

cemeteries across the city fill with visitors setting out candles. The **All Souls' Jazz Festival** (www. deprofundis.dt.pl) takes place over the same week. On November 11, Polish **Independence Day** is marked with a Mass at Wawel Cathedral and wreath-laying at the Tomb of the Unknown Soldier.

WINTER. From early December on, nativity cribs and stalls filled with handmade decorations and local delicacies are set up around the main market square. Masses are held in churches across Krakow on **Christmas Eve,** and on December 25 and 26, both public holidays. The market square fills with revelers on **New Year's Eve**—the next day is a national holiday. Carnival season also begins from January 1, with a series of costumed balls across town, either private parties or organized events in public halls.

The Weather

The local climate is characterized by bitter, long winters, when the temperature can drop to well below freezing, and hot summers, when it can rise to 30°C (86°F) and above. Snow is still common in January and February. The air quality is still affected by Krakow's valley location and proximity to the heavy industry in Silesia and nearby Nowa Huta. The smog can be suffocating.

The wettest times of year are spring and fall—be prepared for sharp showers, particularly in September, the wettest month of the year.

Useful Websites

www.cracow-life.com: Local expat site full of tips and information, big on fun and entertainment.

www.cracowonline.com: Extensive site packed with visitor information. Light on opinion, big on hotel rates and services, tours, and festival details.

www.en.infokrakow.pl: Information resource set up by the Krakow Festival Office, mainly for the promotion of cultural events.

www.jewish.org.pl: These two sites handle all things Jewish in Poland—history, cultural events, and attractions.

www.judaica.pl; **www.krakow-poland.com**: Handy for booking apartments in the city and for finding themed walking tours around it.

www.krakow-info.com: Informative, if somewhat dry, one-stop local database.

www.krakow.pl: The city's official tourism site, with standard information in four languages, including English, and a regularly updated list of cultural events.

www.orbis.pl: Former state-run tourist agency, still useful for the practical aspects of traveling and staying around Poland.

www.poland.travel/en-gb: Useful general site of the U.K. Polish tourist office.

www.poland.travel/en-us: Useful general site of the U.S. Polish tourist office.

Cellphones

World phones—or GSM (Global System for Mobiles)—work in Poland (and most of the world). If your phone is on a GSM system, and you have a world-capable multiband phone, you can make and receive calls from Poland. Just call your wireless operator and ask for "international roaming" to be activated. You can also buy a local SIM card from **T-Mobile** (www.t-mobile.pl), **Orange** (www.orange.pl), or **Plus GSM** (www.plus.pl). Nearly every kiosk in the city center will sell all varieties.

North Americans can rent a GSM phone before leaving home from **InTouch USA** (☎ **800/872-7626;** www.intouchglobal.com) or **RoadPost** (☎ **888/290-1606** or **905/272-5665;** www.roadpost.com).

Car Rentals

Krakow city center is mainly cobbled and pedestrianized—no transport is allowed on the main square. A cheap bus and tram system, and plentiful, inexpensive taxis mean that a car is only necessary if you are going to be making trips in the area—particularly to Ojców or Zakopane. Avis and Hertz both have offices in Krakow. The **Avis** office (Ul.Lubicz 23, ☎ **0601/20-07-02;** www.avis.pl) is near the train station. **Hertz** has an office at the Cracovia Hotel (Al.Focha 1, ☎ **012/429-62-62;** www.hertz.pl), and both have desks at Balice airport (Avis ☎ **012/639-32-89;** Hertz ☎ **012/285-50-84**). Other companies include **EuropCar** (Hotel Qubus, Ul.Nadwiślańska 6, ☎ **012/374-56-96;** www.europcar.pl), also with a branch at Balice (☎ **012/257-79-00**) and **Joka** (Hotel Pugetów, Ul.Starowiślna 13, ☎ **012/429-66-30;** www.joka.com.pl).

Getting **There**

By Plane
Krakow's airport at **Balice** (11km/7 miles west of the city center) has been given the official title of John Paul II International Airport Krakow-Balice. It now has two terminals—terminal 1, for international flights, is currently being expanded, with a new parking lot.

There are three ways to get into town. The easiest is by **train**—a free shuttle bus runs every half-hour from outside Arrivals to the Balice platform. Pay the inspector (6 zł) on the train for the 15-minute journey to the main train station. The service starts at 5:14am and finishes at 10:44pm.

The **292 bus** takes a long route to town.

A **taxi** (☎ 012/19191) costs about 70 zł, the fare rising after 10pm.

By Car
Highway **A2** from Germany runs to just north of Łódź, where it links with the **A1** from Gdańsk and the northern coast. This in turn connects with the **A4/8** from Wrocław, which runs east to Katowice and then Krakow. From Warsaw, drive west to pick up the A1 just north of Łódź then continue south.

By Train
Most national Polskie Koleje Państwowe (Polish State Railway; www.pkp.pl) and international (www.db.de) trains arrive at **Krakow Central** (Pl.Dworcowy 1, ☎ **012/624-54-39**), the main station just east of the Old Town. Half a dozen tram routes stop at Dworzec Główny.

Getting **Around**

By Tram
Trams (www.mpk.krakow.pl) circle the Old Town and link it with the suburbs. They are quick, reasonably frequent, but often crowded. Ticket machines are placed beside almost every stop. A standard single is 2.50 zł, to be stamped on board; 1.25 zł for children 15 and under. Children 3 and under ride free. It costs an extra 0.50 zł to buy a ticket on board from the driver. You can also buy tickets valid for 1 hour (3.10 zł/1.55 zł) and various passes beginning with 24 hours (10.40 zł/5.20 zł).

Note that holders of the **Krakow Card** (50 zł for 48 hours, 65 zł for 72 hours; www.krakowcard.com) are entitled to use city transportation for the length of its validity.

By Taxi
Most journeys around town should cost under 15 zł—the official rate is no more than 7 zł plus 2.80 zł per kilometer between 6am and 10pm, 4.20 zł from 10pm to 6am. Taxis should have their number clearly displayed on the sides and the driver must turn on the meter—rip-offs still exist. **Radio Taxi** (☎ 012/9191) and **City Taxi** (☎ 9621) are reliable.

By Bus
City buses use the same tickets as trams and mainly serve outlying districts. There are also minibuses, such as the no. **100** from Salwator to Kościuszko Mound. There is a limited **night-bus** service (5 zł) too.

By Car

It is hardly worth bringing a car into the city—although many Poles do. Park at a "P" sign and buy a ticket from a passing warden. There is a guarded parking lot at Ul.Westerplatte 18. See p 166 for a list of rental-car companies.

On Foot

Strolling in Krakow is an easy pleasure—the city center is compact, grid-patterned, and quickly negotiated. Key streets Grodzka, Floriańska, and Sławkowska lead to the main market square, Rynek Główny.

Fast **Facts**

APARTMENT RENTALS Scores of companies do long-term rentals in Krakow. You could try: **Krakow City Apartments** (Ul.Szpitalna 34, ☎ **012/431-00-41;** www.krakow apartments.info); **AAA Krakow Apartments** (Ul.Cybulskiego 2, ☎ **012/346-46-70;** www.krakow-apartments.biz); or **Sodispar Service Apartments** (☎ **012/ 423-42-44;** www.sodispar.com).

ATM/CASHPOINTS Maestro, Cirrus, Visa, and MasterCard cards are readily accepted at ATMs all over town—there are half a dozen on and off the main square alone. **Kantor** currency exchange offices are also ubiquitous, with a handful easily found on Floriańska and the main square. Local banks include Bank of Poland, Bank BPH, Bank Ochrony Środowiska, PKO Bank Polski, and Bank Zachodni WBK.

BUSINESS HOURS Krakow keeps the longest hours of any Polish city. While most stick to the regular hours of 10am to 6pm weekdays and 10am to 2pm Saturdays, stores stay open much longer at weekends in Krakow, many in the Old Town and main malls keeping weekday hours. Banks, though, open 8am to 5pm weekdays and 8am to 2pm Saturdays. Many museums close on Mondays. Office hours are generally 9am to 5pm Monday to Friday.

CONSULATES & EMBASSIES U.S. Consulate: Ul.Stolarska 9, 31 043 Krakow (☎ **012/424-51-00;** http://krakow.usconsulate.gov/); **U.K. Embassy:** Ul.Kawalerii 12, 00-468 Warsaw (☎ **022/311-00-00;** http://unkinpoland.fco.gov.uk).

Embassy of Canada: Ul.Jana Matejki 1/5, 00-481 Warsaw (☎ **022/584-31-00;** www.canadainternational.gc.ca/poland-pologne/).

Embassy of Ireland, Ul.Mysia 5, 00-496 Warsaw (☎ **022/849-66-33;** www.embassyofireland.pl).

DOCTORS Ask a Polish speaker to dial ☎ **012/661-22-40** to find your nearest doctor.

ELECTRICITY Poland operates on 220 volts AC (50 cycles), using a two-round-pin plug.

EMERGENCIES For an ambulance or medical emergencies, dial ☎ **999;** for fire ☎ **998;** for police ☎ **997.** The number for all services dialed from a mobile is ☎ **112.**

GAY & LESBIAN TRAVELERS Homosexuality is legal in Poland but public displays of affection between members of the same sex are not as forthright as they would be over the border in Germany. Krakow now has a couple of gay clubs. The lesbian scene is far more underground. See www.gay.pl for more details.

HOLIDAYS National public holidays include: January 1 (New Year's Day); March/April Easter Monday; May 1

(Labor Day); May 3 (Constitution Day); May/June Corpus Christi; August 15 (Feast of the Assumption); November 1 (All Saints' Day); November 11 (Independence Day); December 25, 26 (Christmas).

INSURANCE Check your existing insurance policies before you buy travel insurance to cover trip cancellation, lost luggage, medical expenses, or car-rental insurance. For travel overseas, most U.S. health plans (including Medicare and Medicaid) do not provide coverage, and the ones that do often require payment for services upfront. E.U. citizens may receive reduced or free medical treatment, but must show an EHIC card (U.K.: www.ehic.org. uk; Ireland: www.ehic.ie).

INTERNET Internet access is easily found in cybercafes around the Old Town—most also offer Wi-Fi. A fee of 5zł. should guarantee use of a public computer for an hour. **Garinet** Ul.Floriańska 18, (☎ **012/423-22-33**; www.garinet.pl) is central, reliable, and open until 10pm.

LOST PROPERTY If you've left something on a local tram or bus, try the transportation office at Ul.Jana Brożka 3, ☎ **012/254-11-50.** Call credit card companies (see below) the minute you discover your wallet has been lost or stolen, and file a report at the nearest police precinct. Your credit card company or insurer may require a police report number or record. **Visa's** emergency number in Poland is ☎ **0-0-800-111-1569** (toll free). **MasterCard** holders should call ☎ **0-0800-111-1211** (toll free) in Poland. **American Express** cardholders should call ☎ **1-800-964-8542** in the U.S. or ☎ **+44 1273 696 933** in the U.K.

MAIL & POSTAGE The Polish post office (*poczta*) is reasonably quick and efficient. Post boxes are red. The main office at Ul.Westerplatte

20 (☎ **012/421-03-48;** www. poczta-polska.pl) opens 8am to 8:30pm Monday to Friday, 8am to 2pm Saturday.

MONEY The unit of currency is the **złoty,** usually abbreviated to zł. At press time, the złoty was at its strongest in history, approximately 1 zł to \$0.36 (21p or 24 euro cents).

PASSPORTS No visas are required for E.U. citizens, U.S. or Canadian visitors to Poland providing the stay does not exceed 90 days. If your passport is lost or stolen, contact your country's embassy or consulate immediately; see "Consulates & Embassies" above. Make a copy of your passport's critical pages and keep it separate from your passport.

PHARMACIES You should be able to find a standard pharmacy (*apteka*) open during normal business hours around the Old Town, city center, Kazimierz, and Podgórze. The details of those on 24-hour duty will be displayed in all their windows. **24-hour pharmacy numbers** include ☎ **012/631-19-80** or ☎ **012/265-29-70.**

POLICE The police (*policja*) emergency number is ☎ **997.** The number for all services dialed from a mobile is ☎ **112.**

SAFETY Violent crime in Krakow is rare, street crime occasional. Poorly-lit areas such as the Planty garden ring and around the train station may attract pickpockets after dark but generally the Old Town and Kazimierz are quite safe. Nowa Huta has a bad local reputation but few tourists have any reason to be there at night anyway. There is a **24-hour police station** right on the main market square, at no. 27.

SMOKING In a recent measure, smoking has been banned in public places in Poland, including museums, theaters, bus and train stations, airports, and stadiums. In terms of restaurants and bars, venues may allow customers to smoke in a designated, well-ventilated room—although costs and logistics have so far counted against this provision.

TAXES In Poland, most goods carry a value-added tax (VAT) of 22%. Non-E.U. residents are entitled to a tax refund on goods bought in Poland and taken permanently out of the E.U. within 3 months from the date of purchase. Shops carrying a sticker with the words "Tax Free Shopping" can help reclaim the VAT levy. The customer must revisit the store in question with the original VAT invoice plus the certificate issued at the border or airport when leaving the E.U. Alternatively, agencies such as Global Refund Polska (www.globalrefund.com) do all the paperwork for a certain percentage depending on the purchase amount.

TELEPHONES For national and international telephone inquiries, dial ☎ **912.** For the international operator, dial ☎ **901.** To make an international call, dial ☎ **00,** wait for the tone, then dial the country code, area code, and number. All local calls in Krakow require the three-digit city code first, **012.** To make a long-distance call within Poland, use the relevant city-code prefix first.

TIPPING Only the most exclusive restaurants in town add a tip to the check before it arrives at your table. Otherwise, if you have been satisfied with the service, add the usual 10% or round up to the nearest convenient figure. In cafes and bars, a tip is not expected unless you've been at a place for a long time or the service has been particularly outstanding. For taxi drivers, round up to the nearest convenient figure. A word of warning—if you say "thank you" as you hand over payment, this can be taken to mean that you are not expecting any change back. If that's not the case, make this clear as you pass the waiter the money.

TOILETS Public toilets are more in evidence around the city center these days. In places such as the train and bus stations, there may be a nominal fee to pay an attendant. Pictorial signs almost always differentiate the toilets for men and women.

TOURIST INFORMATION **City Information Point,** Ul.Szpitalna 25 (☎ **012/432-01-10;** www.info krakow.pl) is a little hut in the Planty ring between the Old Town and the train station. It is open daily in summer from 9am to 7pm, and in winter 9am to 5pm. The regional office, **Małopolska Tourist Information,** is on the main market square at Ul.Grodzka 31 (☎ **012/421-77-06;** www.mclt.pl).

TRAVELERS WITH DISABILITIES Krakow is quite limited in accommodating visitors with disabilities. Wheelchair access and lifts have been installed at the train station and a handful of attractions—such as the main building of the National Museum—but the cobbled streets of the Old Town are tricky and few restaurants and only a handful of hotels have been converted.

Krakow: **A Brief History**

50,000B. C. Evidence of human settlement and activity on Wawel Hill.

1ST C. A D Evidence of trade between Krakow settlers and the Roman empire.

600–1000 Pagan Vistulans occupy Krakow for 400 years.

800 Vistulan power and influence wane; Krakow becomes part of the Great Moravian Empire.

1000 Bishopric of Krakow established.

1038 Kazimierz the Restorer makes Krakow the capital of Poland. Construction begins on first cathedral.

1079 Martyrdom of St. Stanysław.

1140s Completion of second cathedral at Wawel. Beginning of first Piast dynasty.

1241 Tartar invasion of Krakow, the first of three. Defensive walls built.

1340s–60s Kazimierz III the Great rules. Wawel rebuilt in Gothic style. Establishment of the University of Krakow.

1389 Jagellonian dynasty established.

1410 The Battle of Grunwald, or Tannenberg. Polish and Lithuanian armies defeat Teutonic Knights. German expansion prevented.

1470s Veit Stoss works on the altar of St. Mary's Basilica. Printing press established.

1491 Nicolaus Copernicus enrolls at the University of Krakow.

1504 Rebuilding of Wawel begins. Zygmunt Bell hung. First Renaissance works in Krakow.

1569 Establishment of Polish–Lithuanian commonwealth.

1596 King Zygmunt Vasa moves the royal court from Krakow to Warsaw.

EARLY 1600s Early baroque style established.

1655 First Swedish invasion of Krakow.

EARLY 1700s Later Swedish invasions.

1734 Last coronation at Wawel.

1772–73 First partition of Poland between Austria, Prussia, and Russia.

1788 Astronomical observatory established.

1795 Third partition of Poland. Krakow becomes part of Austria.

1800 Wawel becomes an Austrian army barracks.

1809 Krakow part of the semi-autonomous Duchy of Warsaw under Napoleon.

1815 Congress of Vienna. Poland partitioned once more. Krakow independent and neutral.

1846 Krakow Uprising—city back under Austrian rule.

1850 Great Fire of Krakow.

1890s Słowacki Theater opens. Flowering of the arts in Krakow. Modernism and the Młoda Polska movement influential.

1901-05 Palace of Art opens. Stary Theater re-opens in Art Nouveau style. Premiere of "The Wedding" by Stanisław Wyspiański.

1914 Outbreak of World War I. Polish legions march out of Krakow. Fighting in Galicia.

1918 Austrian Army disarmed in Krakow. Establishment of Polish independence on November 11 after 146 years of foreign rule.

1935 World War I hero Piłsudski given a state funeral in Krakow.

1939 Nazi invasion of Poland, followed quickly by the Soviets. Occupation of Krakow. Professors and intellectuals rounded up and transported to a concentration camp at Sachsenhausen.

1941–2 Establishment of Jewish Ghetto. Development of a death camp at Auschwitz. Oskar Schindler begins employing a significant number of Jews at his factory. Establishment of a work camp at Płaszów.

1943 Liquidation of the Jewish Ghetto.

1945 Soviet troops enter Krakow. After the war, Krakow businesses nationalized, opposition leaders imprisoned.

1949 Construction of Nowa Huta begins.

1979 Karol Wojtyła becomes Pope John Paul II.

1980–1 Solidarity movement established. Protests in Nowa Huta. Martial law declared. Solidarity banned.

1989 Round Table agreements between Communists and Solidarity. Poland leaves Soviet block. Lech Wałęsa elected leader.

1991 Warsaw Pact dissolved.

1999 Poland joins NATO. Papal visit to Krakow.

2004 Poland joins the European Union.

2005 Mass mourning for the passing of Pope John Paul II.

2010 A plane carrying Polish president Lech Kaczyński and nearly 100 high-ranking Polish officials crashes in fog near Smolensk, Russia, killing all on board. It was en route for a ceremony to mark the 70th anniversary of the Katyń Woods massacre. A state funeral is given for Kaczyński and his wife at St. Mary's Basilica, before burial at Wawel Cathedral.

2011 Poland assumes 6-monthly Presidency of the Council of the European Union.

2012 Poland to co-host soccer's Euro2012 with the Ukraine. Krakow has reserve city status.

Krakow's **Architecture**

Romanesque (11th–12th c.)
Original, intact buildings in the Old Town display pristine evidence of this Early Medieval period—most notably **St. Adalbert's** church in the main market square and **St. Andrew's** church on nearby Grodzka.

Gothic (12th–16th c.)
Gothic emerged in Krakow in the 12th and 13th centuries. The finest example is **St. Mary's Basilica** on the main market square, built around the Romanesque original. The **Dominican Church,** begun in 1250, and **St. Catherine's** in

Kazimierz are further examples. On the northern edge of the Old Town, the **Barbican** and the **Floriańska Gate** show secular use of this architectural style.

Renaissance (early 16th c.)
Italian masters invited to Krakow brought with them the culture of the Renaissance. The most striking example is the arcaded courtyard of the **Royal Castle** at **Wawel. Wawel Cathedral,** originally Gothic, also displays Renaissance touches with the **Zygmunt Chapel,** mausoleum of the Jagellonian dynasty. In the Old Town, the

Sukiennice in the middle of the main market square shows architectural hallmarks of the Renaissance.

Baroque (17th–18th c.)

Italian masters were also responsible for the prevalence and quality of baroque architecture in Krakow. Completed in 1619, the **Church of Sts. Peter & Paul** in Grodzka is early baroque at its best—the High Altar and stucco ceiling above are as magnificent as any baroque creations in Poland. Constructed later that century, **St. Anne's** in the University Quarter provides further evidence.

Modernist (early 20th c.)

Work by the key designers and painters of the Młoda Polska movement—**Stanisław Wyspiański** and **Jan Matejko**—can mainly be seen in ecclesiastical interiors such as the **Franciscan Church.** The **Hotel Pollera** also contains beautiful Art Nouveau glasswork. The best overall architectural example from this period as a whole is the **Palace of Art** on the edge of the Planty by Plac Szczepański.

Socialist & Contemporary (20th c.)

Nowa Huta was laid out according to Socialist planning and retains its features of broad, straight avenues radiating from a central square. Architectural facades borrow from the Renaissance—note the arcaded buildings of Aleja Róż. Also in Nowa Huta, the **Arka Pana** Church shows a bold, contemporary style with its roof in the shape of Noah's Ark.

Useful Phrases & Menu Terms

Useful Words & Phrases

ENGLISH	POLISH	PRONUNCIATION
Good day	Dzień dobry	djyen' dobri
How are you?	Jak się Pan/Pani ma?	yak siye pan/pani ma?
Very well	Bardzo dobrze	bardzo dobrzhye
Thank you	Dziekuję	djye-kuye
You're welcome	Proszę	proshye
Goodbye	Do widzenia	do vidjenya
Please	Proszę	proshye
Yes	Tak	tak
No	Nie	nye
Excuse me	Proszę Pana/Pani	proshye pana/pani
Where is . . . ?	Gdzie jest ?	gdzhye yest?
To the right	Na prawo	na pravo
To the left	Na lewo	na levo
I would like . . .	Poprozę	po-pro-zhye
I want . . .	Potrzebuję	po-trje-buye
Do you have . . . ?	Czy Pan/Pani ma…?	chi pan/pani ma…?
How much is it?	Ile kosztuje?	il-lair kosh-tooye?
When?	Kiedy?	ki-yedi?
What?	Co?	tso?
There is (Is there . . . ?)	Czy jest?	chi yest?

ENGLISH	POLISH	PRONUNCIATION
What is there?	Co jest?	tso yest?
Yesterday	Wczoraj	vchoray
Today	Dzisiaj	dji-see-ay
Tomorrow	Jutro	yutro
Good	Dobry	dobri
Bad	Niedobry	nye-dobri
Better (Best)	Lepiej (Nalepiej)	lye-pee-yey (na-lye-pee-yey)
More	Więcej	vee-yes-sey
Less	Mniej	mn-ee-yey
Do you speak English?	Czy Pan/Pani mówi po angielsku	chi pan/pani moo-vee po an-geel-skoo?
I speak a little Polish	Mówię mały Język polski	moo-vee ma-wee ye-zik pol-ski
I don't understand	Nie rozumiem	nye ro-zoo-mee-yem
What time is it?	Która godzina?	kt-oora god-zina?
The check, please	Poproszę o rachunek?	Po-proshye o ra-hoo-nek?
The station	Dworzec	dvor-zets
A hotel	Hotel	ho-tehl
The market	Rynek	ree-nek
A restaurant	Restauracja	rest-ow-rah-see-ya
The toilet	Toaleta	toe-a-ley-ta
A doctor	Doktor	dok-tor
The road to . . .	Droga do...	dro-ga do?
A room	Pokój	po-koo-ye
A book	Książka	ks-ya-yonzh-ka
A dictionary	Słownik	swov-nik

Numbers

NUMBER	POLISH	PRONUNCIATION
1	jeden	ye-den
2	dwa	dva
3	trzy	tzhi
4	cztery	chteri
5	pięc	pi-yench
6	sześć	shesh
7	siedem	sye-dem
8	osiem	os-yem
9	dziewięć	dj-ye-veech
10	dziesięć	dj-ye-seech
11	jedenaście	ye-den-ash-che
12	dwanaście	dva-nash-che
13	trzynaście	tzhi-nash-che
14	czternaście	chter-nash-che
15	piętnaście	pee-yet-nash-che
16	szesnaście	shes-nash-che

NUMBER	POLISH	PRONUNCIATION
17	siedemnaście	sye-dem-nash-che
18	osiemnaście	osyem-nash-che
19	dziewiętnaście	dj-ye-nash-che
20	dwadzieścia	dva-djee-sheeya
30	trzydzieści	tzhi-djee-shee
40	czterdzieści	chter-djee-shee
50	pięćdziesiąt	peech-djee-shee-yont
60	sześćdziesiąt	shesh-djee-shee-yont
70	siedemdziesiąt	sye-dem-djee-shee-yont
80	osiemdziesiąt	os-yem-djee-shee-yont
90	dziewięćdziesiąt	djee-veech-djee-shee-yont
100	sto	sto

Menu Terms

POLISH	ENGLISH
Śiadanie	Breakfast
Obiad	Lunch
Kolacja	Dinner
Wegetariański	Vegetarian
Jadłłopis	Menu
Talerz	Plate
Nóż	Knife
Widelec	Fork
Łyżka	Spoon
Filiżanka	Cup
Szklanka	Glass
Gotowany	Boiled
Z rusztu	Grilled
Nadziewany	Stuffed
Pieczeń	Roast meat
Mięso	Meat
Ryby	Fish
Drób	Poultry
Zupa	Soup
Ryż	Rice
Ziemniaki	Potatoes
Pierogi	Dumplings with various fillings
Chleb	Bread
Warzywa	Vegetables
Surówka	Salad
Desery	Desserts
Naleśniki	Pancakes
Cielęcina	Veal
Dzik	Boar
Gęś	Goose

POLISH	ENGLISH
Gołębki	Rice and meat in cabbage
Indyk	Turkey
Kaczka	Duck
Kurczak	Chicken
Łosoś	Salmon
Pstrąg	Trout
Wierprzowe	Pork
Wołowe	Beef
Ciastko	Cake
Lody	Ice cream
Pierniki	Soft gingerbread cookies
Sernik	Cheesecake
Cukier	Sugar
Herbata	Tea
Kawa	Coffee
Mleko	Milk
Piwo	Beer
Sok	Juice
Wino	Wine
Wino słhodkie	Sweet wine
Wino wytrawne	Dry wine
Woda	Water
Woda mineralna	Mineral water
Wódka	Vodka

Soups & Stews

POLISH	ENGLISH
Barszcz	Beetroot soup
Chłodnik	Sour milk, beef, and dill soup (cold)
Fasólka po Bretońsku	Bean soup with bacon
Żur	Rye flour soup . . . with sausage and egg
Żurek ż	. . . with potatoes and mushrooms

Dishes of Southern Poland

POLISH	ENGLISH
Kwaśnica	Sauerkraut and meat stew
Oscypek	Hard, salty, local cheese
Strudel jabłkowy	Apple strudel
Zalewajka	Potato, sausage, and mushroom soup

Index

See also Accommodations and Restaurant indexes, below.

Photo **Credits**

Notes